MASTERING
THE VIRTUAL
SALE

Also by Kerry Johnson

New Mindset, New Results

Why Smart People Make Dumb Mistakes With Their Money

Willpower

Mastering Self-Confidence with NLP

Phone Sales

Sales Magic

How to Read Your Client's Mind

Peak Performance

Trust-Based Selling

The Referral Mindset

MASTERING THE VIRTUAL SALE

7 STRATEGIES TO EXPLODE YOUR BUSINESS IN THE NEW ECONOMY

Kerry Johnson,
MBA, Ph.D.

Published 2021 by Gildan Media LLC
aka G&D Media
www.GandDmedia.com

FIRST EDITION 2021

Front Cover design by Tom McKeveny

Interior design by Meghan Day Healey of Story Horse, LLC

Library of Congress Cataloging-in-Publication Data is available upon request

ISBN: 978-1-7225-0552-3

10 9 8 7 6 5 4 3 2 1

Contents

Introduction

COVID-19 Changed Everything

When COVID-19 hit the United States in February 2020, business soon stopped around the world. The only observable transactions were essential establishments such as grocery stores, gas stations, and hospitals. When Trump Administration Vice President Mike Pence announced from the Oval Office in 2020 that the US economy would shut down for fifteen days, everybody was scared but understood the need to stay home. Hospitals would be overwhelmed. Millions would die on the streets if the illness spread too far.

After two weeks, the shutdown was extended to forty-five days, and most realized this was going to be a longer-term pandemic. Forty-five days extended in many states to eighteen months destroying more than 36 percent of customer-facing businesses like restaurants, gyms, hair salons, and bars. That was the situation by March 2021. As of this writing, the economy has slowly reengaged. But lasting changes in the way business is conducted are the result.

Client-facing businesses as well as many others were scrambling to adapt. They did everything possible to survive including wearing masks, installing barriers, and even buying massive shelters for outdoor service. While many restaurants and bars went out of business permanently, many have adapted. Some even thrived. Those that survived learned a new way of connecting. They discovered a way of maintaining engagement and even found their sales could increase.

How Long Will the Virtual Sale Be with Us?

How long will we be conducting business virtually, or is business virtually part of the new normal? In the beginning of 2020, many of us thought the pandemic would last until the end of summer 2020. But as months dragged on, lockdowns progressed. It became apparent that the pandemic would be with us for more than a year. There were some windows of face-to-face opportunity in early summer 2020. But by the fall, many locations were required to lock down.

In a *Wall Street Journal* article at the time, the writer speculated that corporate business travelers were flying much less frequently than in prior years. Leisure flyers were still visiting relatives and taking short vacations. International travel to Europe was prohibited for more than a year. Many experts believe that business travel will recover to about 36 percent of what it was pre-pandemic. While this was terrible news for the airlines, it also meant that doing business virtually is with us to stay. Even after the pandemic is behind us, most meetings will be filtered by a layer of scrutiny to see if they are truly necessary.

Virtual meetings are obviously much less expensive than airline travel to a distant city. It will take some time before companies realize closing ratios have taken a pandemic hit. Most salespeople suffer from their inability to meet face-to-face. Marginal revenue sales calls may never recover. High-ticket sales are indispensable and will recover the fastest.

The *WSJ* article estimated that the loss from sales trips was about 20 percent of a company's income. Conventions and trade shows continue to snap back much faster since they are seen as efficient ways of meeting new prospects and clients.

The airline model of depending on business travel for profits has taken a hit. There was already a move by major carriers like Delta, United, and American to operate more like discount carriers such as Southwest, Spirit, and Frontier. The no-frills airlines were already operating at much less cost than legacy carriers. As mainline carriers attracted fewer business travelers, there were fewer upgrades, smaller seats, and generally less comfortable airplanes. This was in response to less business demand and lower marginal income. There was even talk by one of the big discounters of selling standing seats for flights of less than two hours—one more way of packing passengers in like sardines.

The same innovation cannot be said of many salespeople. I'm a business coach working with small business owners in nearly every industry. It's amazing how many clients became paralyzed at the beginning of the 2020 pandemic.

One company based in Dallas had looked for new business solely by booking appointments at estate planning seminars. But in a COVID-19 environment, few prospects were willing to attend in-person seminars. The company was paralyzed, not able to produce enough new sales.

I suggested to the president and chief executive a way to bypass seminars and generate new sales from their client database of 30,000. The process was simple. They needed to keep in contact with their current clients. I taught the thirty-plus sales force a way to call every three months. The skill set was called the Three-Month Phone Call Script.

It worked like a charm. Those sales producers who were disciplined in using the script effectively closed 38 percent of all prospects they spoke to. It was a raving success. It was an answer to surviving the crisis. But only five or six of the thirty were disciplined enough to dial. The president was enthusiastic about calling clients. He even celebrated the concept on a weekly conference call, but that was it. The culture of the company had been to see prospects face-to-face. When the world changes, sales strategies must adapt.

I coached ten groups of three participants on each call. One of the attendees was emblematic. I introduced the Three-Month Phone Call Script to Jim who was enthusiastic. He committed to calling three clients per day, no matter what. When I followed up on his progress the next week, he only produced excuses. Each week he promised to make the calls. On one coaching call, he pushed back that nobody would answer the telephone. When I pressed him to make more dials the fourth week, he ran out of excuses. I realized that Jim was unwilling to make the calls, even though a third of his colleagues had sales increases of 38 percent using the same method.

As result, ten of the salespeople were terminated for lack of production. Another ten saw their income decrease by half, while the remaining third noticed dramatic increases in their income compared to before the pandemic. Even though the telephone has been with us since Alexander Graham Bell, it's a resource that could have saved the jobs of two-thirds of this sales force.

When a new client starts coaching with me, I'm always amazed at how poorly they sell on the telephone. I'm also shocked at how sophomoric they are on video calls. It's almost as if they were learning how to sell all over again. There are lots of reasons for this virtual phone and video paralysis. Some resistance exists because of call reluctance (like Jim's) while others are blocked by their fear of change.

Underlying the mastery of the virtual sale is your willingness to do something that could be uncomfortable. Conversely, it is also sped by your desire to try something new. Gaining success with the virtual sale depends on your eagerness to take a risk in the hope of high reward, because surely it will come. There is only a slow slide to redundancy without these skills.

Virtual Sales Mistakes

At least 50 percent of my coaching calls every day are made using video, while the rest are by phone. It's amazing how amateurish people are while using video. Some look at the corner of their desk during a call. Other callers are lighted poorly. Faces are often hidden. Many have an internet connection that is so slow that every third word drops off. Images are undefined and annoyingly pixelated.

The virtual sale is a new skill set. It is a cross between selling on a face-to-face platform and applying new ways to communicate. It is not an extension of what you've always been doing. It's a new set of skills. It's a new paradigm to help you not only survive in any environment, but to thrive.

I wrote this book because of the opportunity to help my own clients increase sales by communicating better on any platform and in any environment. A lot has been written on how to log onto a virtual call. You can even read some info on how to record the call. Zoom, Webex, and even Microsoft Teams all have tutorials on how to operate the software. But there's more to making a sale than operating the technology proficiently.

I spoke to one sales pro in Toronto who was in fear of getting terminated from his company. He was a fairly new hire pre-COVID, but couldn't quite adapt to the virtual environment. Our first call by telephone lasted twenty minutes. He was surprisingly verbal. I listened intently. Our second call was on a Zoom platform. It was then I understood why he was challenged. The audio was so bad that I could only hear every third word. The video was pixelated and distracting. But the worst part was his intense need to talk. It was good for me to hear about his goals during the first meeting. But the second appointment was his time to listen.

When I presented coaching options and asked for his thoughts, he replied with excuses. Here's a sales producer struggling to survive while thinking he can talk his way out of any problem. He needed to listen for solutions. Instead, he was doomed to make the same mistakes over and over. I felt bad for the employee, but even if I had worked with him for free, he never would have implemented the changes necessary to survive.

This book assumes that you have a growth mindset. You are willing to change. You are willing to learn new processes, systems, and strategies. You are also willing to implement them. If you do, you will join the 5 percent who are able to make lasting, successful changes just by reading a book. However unique this opportunity, it's up to you to implement what you read to hit your sales goals.

It's important to weave honed sales skills with emotional intelligence. Then overlay the skills on a virtual platform in closing business. In my coaching practice, a particularly specific challenge is to separate product skills from emotional intelligence skills. When salespeople first start, the product benefits are everything. When they realize closing ratios are not what they hoped for, they understand they need sales skills. But rarely do most sales pros understand that prospects don't sell themselves. It's not based on what the salesperson presents. It is focused on how the prospect perceives the information.

Most of the sale is about rapport and trust. There is no possible way of presenting a successful product solution without engendering trust. It is the emotional intelligence of listening,

repeating needs back, and gaining commitment that produces
high closing ratios.

How We Got Here

In 1876, Bell tested his new invention by saying, "Mr. Watson,
come here. I want to see you." It wasn't until the 1940s that the
phone was used as a sales tool to originate new business. In the
1960s, AT&T developed an amazing piece of technology called the
Picturephone. It was simply a videophone using the same slow line
as its voice cousin. At the same time, US presidents started using
video in the Situation Room of the White House using the same
Picturephone technology. But by that time, speeds had increased
using T-1 lines at a blazing 1.5 Mbps.

One of the first public uses of the internet in the 1990s was
using the same slow telephone line with the rocket speed of
56,000 bytes per second. I remember putting my phone on a special cradle that would translate tones into signals my computer
would recognize. Needless to say, it would take nearly five minutes
for simple fields to populate. Five years earlier, I had purchased a
new fax machine using a telephone modem. While cumbersome
to use, it would transmit documents. It was certainly faster than
snail mail.

I was booked to speak at a five-city tour in Australia that year.
I had not received the speaking contract and was getting nervous.
I didn't want to be on the hook for the $3,000 airfare without a
signed contract from the promoter. I remember it took nearly
an hour to transmit the contract to their fax machine. And how

expensive it was to use AT&T international rates. Plus, the time it took to receive a signed contract.

In 2003, Skype enabled all of us to make international calls at a fraction of the price. Soon, Skype added a sketchy video service. But in a couple of years, Skype video was good enough for a virtual conference. As internet speeds increased, so did video quality. Today, Skype is a top-quality audio platform. But it still lacks the visual acuity of Zoom, Webex, and others.

Starting in 2016, I spend about one month per quarter in a little Portuguese town called Carvoeiro. My wife, Merita, is an American Airlines flight attendant and works internationally every week. About ten years ago, we decided to take a one-week vacation every three months somewhere around the world. We have been to Belize, Brazil, Mexico, Italy, and much of Asia. But it wasn't until our one-week holiday in Carvoeiro that we fell in love with Portugal. After four years of renting, we finally bought a home on a cliff overlooking the ocean. While the timing was not good since COVID-19 would hit six months after our purchase, it is still our home away from home.

Before and now after COVID-19, I still work at our southern Portuguese home every day from 2:00 to 7:00 p.m. local time. I use Skype on all audio calls. But video is always best with Zoom. Even in little remote Carvoeiro, internet speeds are 50 Mbps down and 10 Mbps up. This goes to show that we really can do business nearly anywhere in the world.

At my home in California, cable modem speeds are nearly 350 Mbps down and 30 Mbps up. But since no internet connection is foolproof, cell phone serves as a handy backup. My Google Pixel

2 XL smartphone died in 2020. I replaced it with a Pixel 4a (5G) phone. While early in the 5G rollout, speeds were still impressive. As with many providers, Verizon offers unlimited data and fast hotspot speeds in case all else fails.

Virtual Video Was Progressing

The upshot of this limited tech history is that various communication platforms have been slowly building over the last decade leading to the virtual sale we use today. COVID-19 just quickened the process. When we were unable to visit face-to-face, our use of video increased. We will never return to the amount of face-to-face interaction we had during prepandemic days. In-person interaction will never disappear. But after 2020, it will be much more selective. Face-to-face interaction will be relegated to more sophisticated and bigger sales. We still can and will connect in front of people, but only at the end of the sales process that is worth the travel time.

After World War II, many veterans found jobs as salespeople. Even the late Zig Ziglar, one of my mentors, started his career selling pots and pans, door to door. Even shoes, post-1945, were sold on doorsteps. Just as products became less profitable in that environment, face-to-face sales gave way to the phone.

In my audiobook *Tele-Sales: How to Get Business on the Telephone*, I discuss windshield time. This is the amount of time spent driving to each face-to-face appointment. Depending on the location, most salespeople can see three to five prospects per day, driving to each appointment. By using phone or video, that activity can be tripled.

When I first started my career in 1981, I could potentially see three prospects per day. But if one or two canceled at the last minute or stood me up, the day would be wasted. The virtual sale prevents that downtime. I can prospect using my landline or cell when I want and schedule video meetings every thirty minutes, if necessary. The bottom line is I can stay much more productive in a virtual sales environment. Perhaps it took a pandemic to shake us out of the status quo, but the result is a business environment that is much more productive than before.

One Silicon Valley start-up had blown through the initial angel funding years ago. It was now on the third round, but still not profitable enough to take public. Then COVID-19 happened. The workforce couldn't go to the office and thus worked remotely. Travel stopped and forced executives to communicate via Zoom. Conferences to distant locations and retreats stopped. But then something positive happened.

The start-up became profitable. Sales stayed the same. Expenses dropped like a rock. Management is even thinking of relocating to Texas to save taxes. After all, the workers can be productive anywhere. This is why the virtual sale is here to stay. It is just too efficient to abandon. We are all tired of a commute from the bedroom to the living room. But some version of that is our future. Perhaps we will go to the office on Wednesdays. Perhaps every other week. But the virtual environment is permanent. Embrace working remotely. Embrace the virtual sale. The faster you can learn this new environment, the more successful you will be.

Many Clients Are Paralyzed

One of the barriers to the virtual sale is your acceptance of change. Video platforms are new. Using them effectively takes skill and ability. Often this new environment is intimidating. You have to learn to present yourself.

Many of my clients prospected by using seminars in a pre-pandemic environment. When COVID-19 hit, they had no idea how to generate new leads. Some enterprising clients did webinars exactly like seminars. They tried to attract people to a virtual conference using a sexy title and delivering a nonstop forty-five-minute speech hoping the attendees would book appointments. But since there was little interaction or engagement with viewers, most prospecting webinars failed to book any appointments at all. And if they did book appointments, cancellations were substantial.

When you've done a few of these webinars, even on Facebook platforms, the cost is often $3,000 apiece. It's easy to get paralyzed not knowing how to lead-generate without seminars. A virtual video webinar doesn't have the forgiveness or interaction of a face-to-face meeting. When you are in a room with thirty other people delivering a speech, you can get away with a PowerPoint presentation rattling off five or six concepts. But when you deliver in a virtual video environment, not only do your speaking skills have to be stellar, creating any interaction is much more challenging. You need to engage attendees by name every five minutes, use stories at the right moment, and use incentives to book appointments.

Few people have an ability to succeed at this new skill set. It's one more reason why many are paralyzed and intimidated in a virtual sales environment. When you are face-to-face and looking a prospect in the eye, you at least can develop rapport. But your skills need to be much more effective in a virtual environment.

One coaching candidate in June 2020 was convinced he could advertise on Facebook to get thirty people to attend a retirement seminar. The promoter told him 50 percent would book appointments with few cancellations. The cost would be $3,000 per seminar. The candidate was convinced this would be the answer to his prospecting and lead-generation worries. He had no need of working with me since he bought into the seminar promise hook, line, and sinker.

I checked in with him about a month after the seminar and asked about results. To say he was deeply disappointed would be an understatement. Instead of thirty attendees, he had fifteen. Instead of seven booked appointments, he had three. Two canceled, leaving him with one appointment that wasn't even qualified. He wasted $3,000 thinking he could do a seminar the same way he had done face-to-face events at a restaurant offering a free dinner. We're in a different environment. Your virtual seminar skills may need not only upgrading but also relearning.

Intimidation Factor

During the pandemic, many clients didn't want to meet face-to-face fearing infection. The world adjusted to searching for a way to do business without being in the same room. As time went on, it became apparent many prospects wanted to push back meeting face-to-face until the time was right.

There was talk of a vaccine passport proving to others that you weren't a risk of spreading contagion. This gave way to airlines requiring the COVID-19 test before boarding an international flight. One of my coaching clients said one prospect was so desperate for human interaction that he invited my coaching client to meet on the front porch of his home, asking only that both wear face masks. Sitting six feet away, they were able to communicate. But since neither could read facial expressions because of the masks, the interaction was still awkward. It's hard to read body language when most of what you see is a face mask.

I saw a documentary about the 1918 Spanish flu pandemic. Unlike COVID-19, there was never a vaccine created. Herd immunity is generally thought of as antibodies present in 70 percent of the population. This means when 70 percent become infected, the spread of a disease or virus generally stops. But in 1919, the Spanish flu no longer had the contagious impact it did one year before. A person who lived during that time said it wasn't until four years later that people felt comfortable in a face-to-face environment without wearing masks. It was 1923 when people were able to congregate comfortably.

For us, it is likely to be 2024 before the face-to-face sales environment will again become common practice. In-person sales will always be here, just less often. US immunologist Dr. Anthony Fauci warned in 2020 that we may never shake hands again. What all this means is that we will go back to a face-to-face, interpersonal sales environment, just not as often. One-on-one meetings in the same room will be relegated to higher level, higher profit sales opportunities only.

In the 1980s, a particularly persuasive United Airlines commercial aired. One company CEO gathered executives and sales team members into a room. He handed out airline tickets to each, recommending they visit current clients. When one salesperson asked why, the CEO said they lost a key client relationship because they failed to keep in contact. He would never let that happen again. When asked where the CEO was going, he said to visit the lost client.

The commercial was a poignant commentary on the power of relationships. In the future, we will meet on special occasions when there is great opportunity and high chance of sales success. When a US president visits a foreign head of state to conclude a deal, it is usually ceremonial. The secretary of state and other bureaucrats have already done the legwork pounding out details of the negotiation. The heads of state are usually only there to ink the deal. Our future sales environment will be a version of that reality. Much of the sale will be virtual. While the final touches on bigger deals are likely to be face-to-face, much of how you sell in the future will be virtual.

COVID-19 Sped Things Up

COVID-19 quickened the pace of virtual sales. The pandemic demanded electronic communication in lieu of face-to-face. That was a good move. It forced us to be more productive, engaging in much higher sales activity. It's up to you to learn how to sell in this new virtual world. Virtual sales requires that you communicate more effectively. The question is how can you probe, present, and close without physically being there? Since 82 percent of communication is nonverbal, the virtual sale is much more challenging than face-to-face. In the following chapters, I give you a step-by-step process on how to close virtually and effectively.

I'm an Executive Platinum (EP) flyer on American Airlines and have been for the last thirty years. An EP flies hundreds of thousands of miles per year and spends $15,000 in airfare to maintain status. Many other airlines are similar in their requirements. I've flown more than three million miles on American Airlines alone. I have flown another two million miles on United and Delta. But my travel will be less, and those other EP colleagues I interact with all estimate they will fly less frequently. Ninety percent of my trips are speaking at conferences. I suspect the meetings industry will not recover for another four years. My EP colleagues all say their travel is dramatically restricted as well. But a few are still flying. Meeting attendance in the future will be much more selective. More preparation will be done before we can meet face-to-face.

In 1985, I flew to Boston for a speech to 250 business owners. I was referred a month earlier to an executive with Cigna, an insurance company. I called Bob Turner, the marketing VP, and asked for a face-to-face meeting while I was in nearby Boston. He was happy to see me, figuring I was not in Boston too often. We met for about thirty minutes. The meeting was finalized by booking me as their speaker for a sales leader retreat six months later.

That type of in-person scenario is unlikely to happen in the near future. More likely an opportunity now would be to talk on the phone for ten minutes, followed by an email. If I'm lucky, a video meeting could be scheduled for the next week, followed by another virtual video meeting with the conference committee. All this would be preceded by learning the date of their conference, whom they used as a speaker previously, the number of attendees, and the topics most needed.

The world has changed. Is it better? Yes. Is it more difficult to conduct business? Possibly. Do we have to learn a new way of communicating and selling in this environment? Absolutely. The faster you learn how to sell virtually, the higher your closing ratio and the more money you will make.

This book is about how to use the new virtual environment in building your sales career. But learning the tech isn't enough. You will also gain new communication skills that will apply to the virtual sale. You will learn how to listen to subtext, segment needs and even how to commit the prospect or client to finding solutions to those needs.

You will learn how to be nearly as persuasive in the virtual environment as you are in face-to-face relationships.

The next seven chapters correspond to the seven strategies to explode your business in the new economy. Shall we begin?

1

The Virtual Sale Is Different

The default mindset of most salespeople is to think of the virtual environment as simply an electronic version of face-to-face. Most think the video communication process is the same except there is a little less chance to recognize body language. It is better than being on the phone, but not as good as face-to-face.

My son-in-law, Benji Hutchinson, is an executive of a major company's US federal government business based in Washington, DC. They sell biometric solutions such as facial recognition. He is a frequent guest on media news programs and even teaches a graduate-level facial recognition class at George Mason University. Part of his job is to attend industry conferences and explain the benefits of facial recognition. He is also under constant attack during media interviews by privacy groups lobbying to prevent the government from using this kind of technology.

Often the industry conferences generate leads for his salespeople. Whenever you see a camera at a TSA airport entrance, or an airline scanning your face before you embark on a flight, facial recognition is being used.

Benji recently told me about an industry conference at which he paid to be an exhibitor. The meeting was completely virtual. The speakers delivered messages using the same video platform you might see with Webex or Zoom. What made this event remarkable was the experience of the many exhibitors. Benji would wait in a chat room for someone to ask about his technology. He spent the better part of three days sitting in front of his computer hoping that someone might show up. This is a typical example of how one event promoter simply took an effective face-to-face platform and overlaid it into an interactive virtual one. It didn't work. The virtual sale is completely different. It's harder to engage. It's tougher to stop someone in the middle of the aisle to ask their name or where they are from while they walk by.

When I exhibited at conferences in the past, we usually brought along a golf putting green and offered a prize for anybody who could sink one of three tries. The face-to-face interaction as prospects walked in the booth to putt can make all the difference. But you can't do the same activity using a virtual platform. Making eye contact with a passerby and asking if they know anything about facial recognition would be an improvement. But waiting three days for a couple of prospects to enter a chat room is a total waste of time.

Could the virtual experience be improved? Of course. The promoter could have allowed each exhibitor to deliver a presentation followed by a question-and-answer period in a separate chat room for thirty minutes. Another effective idea would be to get the phone number and email address of every attendee. Then allow the exhibitors to send out direct mail pieces followed up by a telephone call. Anything except wasting three days watching and waiting by your computer screen.

This is emblematic of what most people do on virtual calls. They simply take the face-to-face model they have been using for the last thirty years and apply it to video. The difference between communicating on video and connecting face-to-face is dramatic. Think of the rapport differences you have noticed between face-to-face and phone. On the phone, your conversations are much more truncated and include more frequent miscommunication. Voice doesn't generate the same level of enthusiasm when you can see someone's face. In this chapter, I talk about the differences between face-to-face, phone, and virtual video formats. You will learn what the challenges are and how to overcome them.

Types of Virtual Platforms

Many webinar platforms have been with us since the advent of the internet. You probably have used Webex when attending webinars. For many years I used Join.Me because it was inexpensive and allowed up to one hundred attendees. Before that, I used GatherPlace because they were one of the few to allow recordings of webinars. Ten years ago, free webinar services were common. The voice quality was mixed. Recordings could be limited to only twenty minutes. Perhaps there was a charge for storage. But even that cost was minimal.

COVID-19 pushed providers to improve the quality of the platforms. We can no longer accept a virtual call being dropped. We might not get another chance to talk to a prospect. It could take weeks to reschedule.

Here are some examples of virtual audio and video platforms that you may be using right now or are considering:

ZOOM

Zoom is one of the easiest platforms to use and relatively the least expensive. You can record, use both video and audio facilities, admit guests into a conference, or even give attendees a password to join when they want. During the pandemic of 2020, Zoom had perhaps the most explosive growth trajectory of any conference platform. It earned a whopping 700 percent growth in its stock price.

Zoom was perfectly positioned to take advantage of the new virtual sales environment. They maximized video quality even with slow internet speeds. For about $15 a month, you can even store 85 MB of video and audio data indefinitely. I use Zoom about four hours every day. I record most of my client calls. I erase those recordings usually after ten days, thinking that if a client didn't listen to the recordings after a week, they never will. I simply warn my clients they have ten days to listen. The next level up is the enterprise version costing two or three times more than the basic rate—but still a good deal for a virtual platform with fine stability.

In October 2018, I made coaching voice calls from my terrace in Carvoeiro, Portugal. I had been using Skype for the past few years.

But for whatever reason, Skype became inconsistent, dropping my calls or making the audio sometimes hard to hear. These problems caused a lot of frustration. My New Jersey client said he could hear a kind of cricket sound during the call, cluing him in that I might be calling from abroad. Once I moved to the Zoom platform, the calls became crystal clear. I never went back to Skype.

GOOGLE MEET

Another platform is Google Meet. As with many products, Google offers a free service trying to hook you into using its platform. Then they increase rates slowly to steer you toward their paid service. It meshes easily with Google Calendar so you receive alerts to scheduled meetings. Both you and your invited callers will be emailed three days ahead and ten minutes before the conference call. Of course, you can adjust these reminders, but they are still helpful.

The only problem is that Google Meet appears as a default in the Google Calendar. You must exit out of Google Meet to prevent the program from notifying your participants to use it. I made a mistake a few times of directing clients to a Google Meet call in error when I failed to exit out.

Fortunately using platforms like Zoom and Google Meet are not all that difficult. Zoom provides a convenient extension for Google Calendar. But you still have to exit out of Google Meet.

MICROSOFT TEAMS

Microsoft Teams has become the de facto platform for internal collaboration. This vertical market brand has become the go-to platform for enterprise conference solutions. Salesforce recently paid $29 billion to acquire Slack's business communication platform in an attempt to compete with Microsoft Teams. It is widely expected that Salesforce (a cloud-based software company) will broaden the platform to directly compete with Zoom, Webex, and others.

WEBEX

Webex is another popular virtual audio and video platform. While not as popular as Zoom, it has been a staple many more years than Zoom. Webex tends to be more cumbersome. It is also not as effective for one-on-one conference calls. It doesn't deliver the same picture quality at slower internet speeds. I like Webex for larger webinars because it displays an attendance counter showing how many are on the call. I constantly find myself checking whether any attendees drop off during the call. I can see in real time whether I am holding the group's attention. I rarely lose more than 5 percent of attendees on a Webex webinar. But when I do lose somebody, I notice it.

Zoom and Webex cost about $15 a month for small business use and are free if you want minimal service.

Nearly all the audio and video platforms are inexpensive. There is no reason why cost should be a barrier to you selling virtually.

Prices have decreased dramatically over the last ten years. My go-to platform during the last decade was Join.Me. It was nearly $80 a month just a few years ago. Surprisingly, that cutting-edge platform didn't hold a candle to the technology available today at one-fifth the price. Even if your company is unwilling to pay for a virtual connection, you will still be able to get the best platform even if you have to pay out of your own pocket.

In picking a virtual platform, it's important to select not only the best price, but also the best value. This means flawless audio, crisp video, and, of course, the ability to record your calls. For example, I like nearly any microphone or speaker set-up on Zoom. It all works. I can put a microphone into my 3mm slot, use a type C connection, or even a USB 3.0. It all connects flawlessly. But when using Webex, you need to plan on at least thirty minutes of experimentation to see what sound connectors will be accepted.

While Webex, Skype, and Join.Me are all excellent platforms, ease of use is as critical as the quality of the call. Plus, if you are having trouble connecting, your prospect or client may have the same difficulty.

Many of my coaching clients work with seniors over sixty years old. While twenty- and thirty- somethings are technologically adept, it's hit and miss with older folks. Some who spent their lives as professionals are comfortable with technology while others push back against it. This makes ease of use all the more important. If your prospect or client is over sixty, any platform they are unfamiliar with may cause friction. It's much better to make them comfortable no matter what the communication platform.

For example, one of my clients refused to book an appointment with a provider who wouldn't talk by phone. Instead, he required the client to book time on his calendar before he would engage. This might work for some prospect segments but also may cause friction with others less comfortable with diminished human interaction.

Most of these platforms include a calendar link. For example, when you schedule a Zoom call, a link is produced you can email to your client. All you have to do is click on the link to enter the call or conference. If the process becomes more complex, it may be too challenging. Again, ease of use is paramount.

Communication Differences

COVID-19 has taken us from face-to-face to phone and then leap-frogged directly to video. Obviously, an improvement over voice and audio presents its own challenges. Video can be more distracting, but it also can generate more rapport and engagement. You heard before that 82 percent of communication is nonverbal. That doesn't just mean body language. Nonverbal also refers to voice inflection, pace, pitch, and timbre on the phone. Video just adds more texture and information to the nonverbal communication.

You'll find challenges using any video or audio platform. Unlike face-to-face communication, video and phone engagement tends to be more abbreviated. You must get your point across faster and get more interaction.

How Good Are Your Engagement Skills?

Some techniques you can use to get more engagement are tie-downs and trial closes. Most of us have an attention span between ninety seconds and five minutes. After that, we often lose attention and check text and email messages. We might plan activities for the rest of the day and even daydream.

During one video commercial, basketball player Stephen Curry drove home talking on his cell. After only a few minutes, he became distracted trying to remember what his wife wanted him to buy on the way home. He only listened to every other word during the conversation. Think of this when you do a monologue on a virtual call. If the client can get distracted, they will.

A few years ago, I called a LinkedIn prospect to talk before we connected. I believe LinkedIn should be a relationship, not just a random name in a rolodex. I called at the appointed time. I asked how he connected and what he knew about me. This always gives me the opportunity to do an elevator speech. He became distant. I heard a lot of "ums" and "uh-huhs," unresponsive to my questions. Finally, I said, "If there is a better time to talk, we can reschedule."

The guy said, "I'm sorry. I am just trying to finish an email, and I didn't know you would be asking so many questions." I stopped the conversation and asked him to call me back when he had more time. This is what some people expect from a virtual call now. They allow themselves to become distracted because they know you won't engage them like you would on a face-to-face meeting.

TIE-DOWNS

Your prospects and clients have extremely short attention spans. If you don't engage frequently, they will become distracted and lose interest. One technique to maintain attention is the use of tie-downs. This is phrasing such as "Make sense?" or "Do you agree?" and "Right?" One of my pet peeves is to hear someone use the same tie-down phrases robotically. For example, "Right? Right?

Right?" I want to reach through the phone and grab them by the neck. "Can you please use another phrase?"

Using your prospect's name in a sentence can also be engaging. For example, "My aim in presenting it this way, John, is to not only save you money, but also make it as useful as possible." You don't necessarily have to ask questions every ninety seconds. But it's critical to draw the caller in every five minutes to keep them attentive.

TRIAL CLOSES

While tie-downs are useful mechanisms to keep listeners attentive, trial closes are an effective way to gain commitment. Trial closes can be used in any conversation; they are a way to keep your prospect or client in agreement especially during a virtual sales call. Any technique like this could allow your prospect to interrupt and take the conversation down a rabbit hole. But it's worth the risk to keep them engaged. For example, "It's really important, John, to ensure this technology is going to be effective and scalable. Do you think this might work in your business?"

Remember, the listener always controls the conversation. If you get a question from a client, they are controlling the flow, not you. They have the ability to move the conversation in any direction they want just by the questions they ask.

Many years ago, I was leading a small group of parents in a communication skill-building exercise to engage their teen kids more effectively. Most of the parents were stuck on how frustrating it was to get through to their teens and why they wouldn't listen. I asked the group of parents if they were in control when they spoke to their kids. All said yes.

But, in reality, the teens were in control. They could control the whole interaction just by the questions they asked. Finally, I got the parents to focus more on asking questions instead of telling their kids what to do. Once the parents were able to figure out how to ask questions the teens wanted to hear answers to, it all made sense. The parents finally started to engage. They were able to listen to their kids and get through.

Generally, my virtual coaching calls are thirty to forty minutes. The first ten minutes is spent checking on my client's activity and to make sure they are following our business plan. The next ten minutes is focused on whether they were able to apply new skills from our last call. If there are any questions about the previous week's call, we take time to work out any concerns.

The last part of the call is spent introducing new material. At no time during any call am I lecturing. Talking for more than ninety seconds will not make any changes in my client's behavior. It is easy to lecture. But if I do, the client will listen intently and learn nothing. I use tie-downs every ninety seconds to keep them attentive. I employ trial closes every five minutes to make sure I gain commitment. I want them to get excited and implement new skills so they can use my teachings to improve their business. If they go back to their old behaviors, nothing is accomplished.

You need to do the same. A good mindset is to assume that nobody is willing to listen to you more than five minutes. If you keep that in mind, you will always stay relevant in the conversation. A possible exception is speaking at a conference with a large group of attendees. But even then, you need to engage. Nobody wants to hear a speaker drone on for an hour. They want to engage and participate.

I have been a convention speaker for the last forty years. COVID-19 clipped my travel wings for a time. But the skills that produce a sterling speaker are never forgotten. The skilled convention speakers are the most engaging. Early in my career, I learned to engage audiences every five minutes by asking them to raise their hands in response to questions. I always speak to attendees before presentations and use their names often during the presentation. I feel especially lucky when attendees wear name tags. Either way, I ask questions of every audience and always engage them individually as I walk around the room.

Many years ago, I spoke to 26,000 real estate agents at the MGM Grand Hotel in Las Vegas. I stepped down from the stage into the first row, shocking the audience. No one had ever done that with such a large group. The camera crews were chasing me around the convention hall adjusting the house lights as I walked. It is safe to say, the audience wasn't sleeping at that event. You can see a clip of that speech on my website at www.KerryJohnson.com.

It's easy to keep attention when you're working a room. It's much more difficult to keep people attentive on a virtual call. But you must do it.

Less Is More in Virtual

One aspect of any virtual call is the need to get to the point faster than if you were standing in front of the prospect. When you are face-to-face, there is more of an allowance to talk about weather, family, sports, or even mementos in someone's office. But a virtual call doesn't allow you that luxury. There can always be a little chatting at the beginning of the call. Perhaps the weather is frightful. Maybe you spot something in the background to comment on. But at best you only have a few minutes to get to the point.

When you are face-to-face, a one-hour meeting may boil down to thirty minutes of relevance in accomplishing a goal. But the rapport developed in that hour is important. Chatting about the weather is important in gaining trust. On a virtual call, you still need to establish the same level of rapport. You just need to do it faster. On a virtual call, you only have about a three-minute window to develop rapport.

Every interaction depends on rapport. Rapport generates trust. By talking for a few minutes about your prospect's environment, you are allowing rapport to develop. This will help the call become more fluid between you and the prospect or client. Since the virtual call is more compact, the rapport development period is also shorter.

The way to develop rapport is with an agenda. Be willing to announce how long the call will take, and let the listeners know when there will be time for questions.

Here's a sample virtual conversation:

YOU: "I was thinking about you this week. I heard you are in for a storm. Are you in that snow belt I heard about?"
CLIENT: "Yes, but I don't think it will have much impact. People here get paralyzed even with a few inches of snow or rain. It's crazy."

You: "My agenda today is to talk about the event in June. I
want to work out topics, possible speakers, and location
for the event. I want to be done in forty-five minutes with
any final questions or wrap up and then end by the top
of the hour. Any thought about your agenda before we
start?"

This type of interaction can also be a template. The virtual call is
not only shorter, but also an expectation of what will be accomplished. If your virtual call is one-on-one, it's a good idea to make
sure the prospect doesn't cut you short. For example, after you
state the agenda, ask, "How are you doing on time?"

There is nothing worse than to be in the middle of any call only
to find out your prospect has to attend another meeting. It's always
good to find out what your time limits are before you start.

An example of fleeting attention occurred recently during a
collaborative webinar. Sixty people attended a virtual conference
in which I participated as the expert resource. Three executives
were on the call. The event was called Thirsty Thursdays. At 5:30
p.m., the leaders had various libations in hand including wine,
beer, and cocktails.

I had just landed in Washington, DC, from LA to see my
grandkids. I felt really jet-lagged but was ready for the meeting.
The last thing I needed was to participate in the alcohol proving
how disoriented I was from the flight. The execs chatted for about
ten minutes about their favorite wine and what they would do the
rest of evening. I saw the attendee count drop from sixty to forty

while they were talking about their favorite wine. The audience didn't feel engaged. If I wasn't the speaker, I would have dropped off too.

There was no agenda. There was no mention of how long the event would last. The title of the meeting was "How to Increase Your Closing Rate." At least we had that hook to keep attention.

The lesson is to never let unforced errors happen during your calls. You can do a lot to maintain attention. You can state the agenda at the beginning of the call. You can advertise bullet points to hype the meeting. You can also maintain engagement by using a few of the attendees' names.

I discussed earlier how to keep attention by using tie-downs every ninety seconds. But there are other ways to keep attention. It all starts with realizing there is a five-minute attention barrier. Nothing you can say will cause people to focus longer than that.

One friend is a Washington, DC, lobbyist who seems to be on a constant stream of daily conference calls. Half of her calls are with multiple attendees. I noticed how often she is on mute. She is distracted by reading telephone messages and working on her laptop and other projects. I asked why she even participates in these calls. She says that the calls are important. She wants her colleagues and clients to know she shows up.

But we still need to pick the right places to show up. Some virtual conferences and webinars seem like a waste of time. Don't overcommit. If you are the presenter, either engage the attendees frequently or don't do the call at all.

Even though virtual voice and video calls are not the same as being in person, you can still use nonverbal cues to make your point. There is nothing worse than being on a call with someone who has a droning, monotone delivery.

Few activities are more boring than a video call with someone who rarely makes eye contact. Your voice tone, pace, pitch, and rhythm on an audio call are all important. In a way, you are trying to keep the prospect entertained. The best speakers have vocal variety. They speak loud and soft, fast and slow. One of my professional speaker friends says that you must deliver your message like a blind discus thrower. The bystanders must be kept attentive.

You can do all of this on a virtual call. Not only can you utilize vocal variety, you can also gesticulate your hands, gain attention with your facial expressions, and even smile frequently to make an impact. I watched a silent film many years ago featuring Charlie Chaplin. Despite being limited to black and white, it was amazing how entertaining the film was without a soundtrack. Every few minutes an announcement popped up on the screen informing the viewer what was happening. But the real show was Chaplin's facial expressions and over-the-top eye movements. Without the benefit of sound, he had to be even more skillful to keep attention.

The virtual video sale is the same. You need to compensate by being bigger than life. You need to use more hand gestures. You need to employ more vocal variety. You need to use more tie-downs and trial closes than you would face-to-face. All this maintains attention. This will also give you an edge in becoming much more persuasive and increase your ability to gain compliance during the call.

Trust Is Key

I once heard the definition of trust as being the overwhelming confidence a client has that you will do what's best for them. The opposite happens without trust. This is your rejection of a $100 bill offered by a stranger on the streets of New York City thinking it's a trap. Trust is everything. With trust, I can get people to listen. Without trust, nothing gets accomplished.

Competence is still important. You need to have credibility. But people rarely buy based on just that. You also need to communicate the trust that you will apply competence to do what is best for the prospect or client. The client and prospect must know that you can deliver on promises.

The most important part of any virtual call is first gaining rapport, which leads to trust. Nothing can happen without trust. Deals get accomplished with it.

When I attended graduate school at the University of California at San Diego, I was part of a research team that led a study showing that trust is worth 17 percent of the gross price of a product or service. What this means is that you can increase your prices up to 17 percent without losing business. But without trust, even a 1 percent increase will lose a customer to the competition.

I've spoken a lot about how important it is to gain and maintain trust during the virtual sale. It is much tougher than face-to-face—but just as critical.

The question is this: how can you gain trust quickly during virtual calls? We know that people buy trust first, products and services second.

I spoke at a seminar many years ago and asked the audience why and how do people really buy. I just got blank stares. I then said I would give them a few choices they could pick from. Was it price? Could they just undercut the competition and always get business? Possibly, but someone is always willing to beat your price even if they have to take a loss.

Do customers buy because of speed of delivery like Amazon Prime? Do they buy because they can get double the quality at half the price? At that point during the speech, I usually single out a marketing VP and ask if they will allow the salespeople to cut prices by 25 percent and make up the difference with a higher volume of sales? Nearly every VP politely smiles and shakes their head no. I've actually managed to irritate a few CEOs who thought I was serious.

But then I usually follow up with a simple question. "Please raise your hand if you think that trust is the most important thing that you do?" Nearly everybody responds yes. Then I ask them if they know specifically, pragmatically, step-by-step, exactly how to get trust? No hands go up. Jokingly I say, "Let me get this straight. The most important thing you said you do is trust, and you're not even sure how to do it? Did I get that right?"

Few people know how to get trust aside from platitudes like "be honest" and "show empathy." But you are the exception. You are reading this book.

People buy from people who are similar. We avoid people who are dissimilar. We tend not to trust those we can't predict behavior of. People buy from people who act like them, talk like them, and even look like them. People avoid others they don't share commonalities with.

Let's say that I'm talking to somebody and we have a lot in common. They have grandkids like me, possibly play tennis and golf like me, and even have advanced university degrees. That would be a beginning of a trust-based business relationship, right? But it takes more. Those values and characteristics are a good start. More importantly, the faster way to gain trust is whether you also share the commonality of their voice pace, pitch, rhythm, and tone. People trust people who are like them.

Let me give you an example. If I'm a fast-talking New Yorker on a conference call with somebody who is a slower speaker from Alabama, there will be little rapport in the beginning. If I talk a mile a minute to a colleague in Texas, there could be a mismatch. Therefore, I need to match and mirror what I hear. If my prospect or client speaks rapidly, I need to speed up. If they speak slowly, I need to modulate. People mirror people they trust. They avoid people they distrust.

Early in my career in 1985, I was one of the first researchers to apply neurolinguistic programming (NLP) techniques in business. Two University of California, Santa Cruz, researchers, Bandler (psychologist) and Grinder (linguist) had created a model of how people communicate. One of the easiest applications of this new field was how to get rapport. I couldn't wait to try it out.

At twenty-seven years old, I was on the phone at least five hours a day calling all over the US. I am a naturally fast speaker, but I had no idea how much I mismatched listeners. Based on my new knowledge of NLP, I slowed down when I heard a prospect pause. I sped up when I sensed the prospect had a quick delivery. My sales immediately increased. I could feel the connection. Every conversation seemed to flow better. If this seems far-fetched, you just haven't been paying attention to your virtual conversations. When you generate more rapport, you also engender more trust. When you elicit trust, your sales production increases.

Sometimes, I get the question that matching and mirroring will cause the prospect to feel mocked and diminished. Yes, that could happen if done poorly. For example, if you are a lightning-fast speaker and slow down abruptly for your listener, your change in pace will be noticed. A rule of thumb is to wait five to seven seconds. If you notice your prospect is a fast speaker, speed up your voice pace over the next five to seven seconds. Or you could slow down waiting for the same interval. If you match and mirror more than seven seconds, nobody will ever think you are being disingenuous or manipulative.

Don't get caught up in thinking that the virtual sale (or any other sales process) is all about technical mechanics. You are still in the people business. It's all about rapport and trust. Everything else, if not related to people skills, is tangential and secondary. Don't get mesmerized with the position of the camera or the quality of the microphone. Lighting is immensely helpful, but it still doesn't make up for your ability to maintain human engagement. The interaction is all about the people. It's all about rapport and trust. These are the most important aspects of the virtual sale.

The concept of putting people skills first is especially challenging to those who focus on product knowledge. They revert to what they know. If they aren't educated and confident in their communication skills, they try to overwhelm prospects with product knowledge. It usually doesn't end well. You will never be able to increase your closing ratio unless your people skills are good.

So far, I've outlined how to gain rapport and trust through matching your prospect's voice tone, timbre, pace, and pitch. The more you talk like your prospect or client, the more rapport you will gain and the more trust you will develop.

We are often in a virtual video environment, not just an audio one. We can see as well as hear them. Many of the interpersonal communication skills that are useful in a face-to-face environment are applicable in a virtual one as well. Just as you learn how to match and mirror your prospect's voice, the same can be done with body movement.

When your prospect sits back in their chair in a face-to-face environment, you should also sit back in your chair. If they sit to the side, you should also sit to the side. If they prop their head in their hand, you should do the same.

Match and mirror your prospect even in a virtual setting to gain rapport and generate trust.

Does this work? Absolutely. People gain rapport faster with those who are similar. They avoid those who are unlike them. This rapport applies not only to your background, values, morals, and education, but also to how you communicate. The more you communicate like your prospect or client, the more rapport will be attained. If you maintain rapport long enough, you will generate trust. Trust, everything else being equal, is why people buy.

In 1993 while writing my book *Sales Magic*, I attended a cocktail party the evening before a speech in Pasadena, California. I was nominated by the US Junior Chamber of Commerce (Jaycees) as one of the most outstanding young men in America. I was a newly minted PhD and only a couple of years removed from the pro tennis tour. I also was just beginning my speaking career and must've looked like an easy mark. The Jaycees, a young adult (ages twenty to thirty-five) affiliate of the US Chamber of Commerce, were a nationwide organization always looking for speakers. The problem was they had no budget. While the Jaycees were unable to pay speaking fees, they certainly had lots of free beer. No matter where you looked, a keg was close by. The audience during my speech numbered in the thousands. Of course, there were kegs of beer everywhere in the conference room. This is the one and only time I saw attendees gathered around kegs of beer. Never happened since.

The evening before my speech, I spoke to the president of the group about the event. During the cocktail party, I had a beer in my right hand and was propped against the door jamb with my right shoulder. After my second glass of beer, I noticed the president holding his beer in the same hand as I was, and leaning against a door jamb as well. Since I was so cognizant of matching and mirroring, after the research on my new book, our mutual mirroring hit me like a ton of bricks.

I started to notice the flow of the conversation. We were both having a lot of fun and had great rapport. We could have talked for a couple of hours. The rapport was so thick that one attendee walked in front of us swaying in the hallway, obviously drunk. The president and I raised our eyebrows and glasses at the same time glad that wasn't us.

At that moment, I decided to try something crazy. I purposely mismatched. I moved my left shoulder against the opposite door jamb. I even switched hands holding the beer. I waited to see what the president would do. It took a while, but he unconsciously mirrored me back. What seemed like an eternity, the mirror only took about twenty seconds.

The Trust Check

Once you are in rapport with a client or prospect, you have a natural inclination to maintain it. If you mismatch somebody while in rapport, they will try to mirror you back in an attempt to continue trust. Generally, you can check how much trust you have by purposely mismatching your prospect or client, as I did. Then notice whether they follow. If they mirror you back, you have an enormous amount of rapport. If they don't, go back to mirroring, wait a while, and try to mismatch again.

I received a letter thirty years ago from my client John Milam in Knoxville, Tennessee. John had heard me speak a couple of times and said he was a fan. One day, he showed up at a prospect's office about ten minutes early. The prospect was thirty minutes late, making John wait for nearly forty minutes. As he approached John, both arms were crossed. John immediately crossed his arms in response. The prospect said, "I'm sorry I'm late. But I don't have time to meet with you today."

John said, "No problem. Would you like to reschedule?"

Something clicked in the prospect's head. He said, "How long will it take if I see you right now?"

John said, "Ten minutes, unless you ask me any questions."

They walked back to the prospect's office. He settled into a big wing-backed chair. John sat in a smaller one in front of the desk. The prospect said, "You have ten minutes, go!" After five minutes, the prospect reclined and crossed his fingers behind his head. Guess what John did? You guessed it. John mirrored his prospect. John leaned back and crossed his fingers behind his head mirroring his prospect. John wrote me that they both looked like a couple of plucked chickens.

But then John did something crazy. He leaned forward on the prospect's desk. Dumb, right? John actually invaded his prospect's personal space. Crazy, unless the prospect does guess what? He followed John onto his own desk instead of John continuing to mirror. This is called a trust check. If you mismatch and notice they mirror you back, you have used the trust check to see how much trust you have. If you see this, stop talking. If you keep talking, you will oversell and buy it back.

The application of this technique that you can use during a virtual sale is to first match and mirror. If your prospect speaks quickly, speed up your pace. If your client talks slowly, throttle down after a seven-second interval. Gaining rapport and trust are the two most important aspects of the virtual sale. On a Zoom platform, as with many others, your communication speed, pitch, and pace are important. Your goal to gain rapport is the same as in any other interpersonal mode.

But once you have matched and mirrored your prospect, check how much trust you have from time to time. You can implement this trust check by speaking with a burst of speed and see if the prospect follows. You could also slow down to check whether the client mirrors you back. Using the trust check may seem complex in the beginning. But isn't it worth it to check how much trust you have? Merely employing this skill set will make you a much better listener.

Listening is the first step to making the prospect feel understood. Most research has shown this is the beginning of rapport. At that point trust comes a lot more naturally. After trust, everything else is easy.

In the next chapter I talk about the versatile virtual salesperson. Versatility is defined as your ability to sell on any platform.

2

The Versatile Salesperson

When I first started my speaking and coaching career in 1981, versatility meant communicating in a way your prospect could best understand. At that time, the concept of buying styles—or how people make decisions to buy—was just coming into vogue. The idea was if you could find out what buying style your prospect used, you could sell that way.

An example would be if your prospect was a fast, get-to-the-point kind of buyer, you would need to also bottom line your ideas faster. Today, versatility is defined as not only how you communicate to individual buying styles, but also your mastery of the actual communication process on each platform. Versatility now means that you are as effective on video as audio. Your face-to-face skills also need to be excellent. While video is more engaging than only audio, your video skills need to be nearly as effective as your interpersonal engagement.

Most Americans feel uncomfortable on video. The biggest concern is how they look. Of course, if appearance is important to you when you are face-to-face, it will become even more of a concern using video. Yet, utilizing video should present no more discomfort or anxiety than a face-to-face meeting. If you are likely to be fairly comfortable in person, then why is video so scary?

Do I Look Attractive?

In one study, 59 percent of respondents said they felt less attractive on video than face-to-face. In fact, 48 percent worried more about how they looked on video than about the virtual meeting content. I do a lot of promotion for my books. After sixteen books, I've been on CNBC and Fox News, as well as on many other mass media. Some of the time, various media outlets will put makeup on me. Most of the time, guests are escorted from the green room to the studio with no makeup at all.

I have never liked myself on camera. I always cringe when I have to see my interviews. I hate seeing the bags under my eyes, five-o'clock shadow, my sometimes-blank looks, and tendency to look at the host instead of the camera. The good news is that nobody expects a guest to look as good as the host. More accurately, nobody cares about how I look. They only focus on whether I am interesting, entertaining, and whether I can say something of value.

Radio is a different story. I am evaluated by my voice tone, pace, pitch, and rhythm as well as content. Only after the interview am I evaluated based on looks. The old radio disc jockey joke about having a face for radio still applies. I guess I found the sweet spot since I don't think I look good on camera nor do I sound good on radio. I even hate seeing my video-recorded speeches. But I think I'm in good company since many superstar actors also can't stand seeing themselves on camera either.

All this has nothing to do with reality. You are who you are. You communicate both on camera and video as an individual. In fact, your voice is as unique as your fingerprints. Nobody will walk away from a video meeting thinking you weren't good-looking enough, just as others never left a phone call thinking they did not like your tone or the way you sounded as long as you meant to be polite. Let's take the intimidation factor out of the equation. Just get on the saddle and schedule those video calls. The more you do, the better you will get.

Many years ago, I gave a speech in Detroit at an evening public seminar. The promoter recorded the event to sell later as a seminar series. The audience numbered 200. Before my speech, Michael, the promoter, told me to ignore the audience and speak directly to the camera. He only needed the audience there to make the meeting seem more dynamic.

The problem was me. I was so conditioned to interact with the audience, I couldn't bring myself to make eye contact very long with the camera. Sure, I looked at the lens once in a while. But I would engage the audience 95 percent of the time. That was my style. In retrospect, audience interaction is always better. The more the audience responds, the better the speaker performs. The promoter made five videos from my three-hour speech. They were well done. The content was relevant. My stories were engaging. But

I could have been so much more engaging to video viewers had I interacted with the camera more often.

The same concept should be used when doing virtual video. Not only do we need to make eye contact with the camera, but also become much more engaging than on an audio call. This means you have to fight the temptation to avoid distractions like checking your texts. If you have to use notes, it's much more important to glance down at a sheet of paper and then reengage with your prospect. Video requires much more engagement than an audio call.

In a face-to-face environment, you would prepare yourself with notes to glance at while maintaining eye contact with the prospect. In an audio phone environment, you never have to take your eyes off your notes. Just remember that your prospect is thinking a lot more about themselves than about you. They are much more focused on how they feel than about how you look. This doesn't mean you should dress down or make infrequent eye contact. It does mean that any level of your self-consciousness is also self-inflicted.

Recently I did a virtual webinar called Mastering the Virtual Sale. I used forty-four slides and put notes on them all. I rehearsed twice before the event. I looked at my notes frequently. Had I been face-to-face, I would have memorized the presentation or jotted down one-word memory joggers that would have reminded me of what to say. The point is that you can get lazy presenting in a virtual environment.

But this also means that the virtual platform, especially on video, is about preventing distractions. If you aren't well lit, the viewers can't see you. A slow internet connection may freeze or pixilate your face. Your voice may sound garbled. If your office has kids' toys everywhere, the prospect may be distracted looking at the messy room. You need to be as presentable on video as you would sitting in someone's office. Your goal is to prevent distractions no matter where you are.

Versatile People Can Sell on Any Platform

The virtual sales master is someone who can sell on any platform. When using only audio, you need to make sure to use a landline, call at the appointed time, and ask the right questions. When using a video platform, make sure your face is well lit, minimize distractions in the room behind you, and make sure the connection is fast enough that your mouth syncs with the words coming out of it. Obviously, in a face-to-face environment, you don't have to worry about technical communication issues. But you do have to arrive on time, be prepared, and listen effectively. When you can master communication on the phone, face-to-face, and virtual platforms, you also have versatility. This is your ability to sell anywhere your prospect chooses to be.

Versatility also refers to your ability to listen. Not a day goes by where I don't feel pitched to. When a salesperson calls, they try to sell whether I need the product or not. If I walk into a store and ask about a product, a clerk will tell me to buy it instead of asking what I need it for. It's the rare salesperson who tries to discover needs before they pitch and sell. But this is also the true definition of versatility. The truly versatile virtual sales master not only uses a video or audio platform as a way to communicate, they also realize that true success lies in their ability to listen.

Versatility refers not only to your ability to sell on any platform, but also to your skill in selling to any person. Think of it this way. If all you did was pitch product benefits, you would only be successful with about 10 percent of your prospects. Actually, that is a fairly high percentage, because you are only guessing at who is going to be interested. But if you listen to needs first, you can tailor product benefits to what they want to hear. If you listen to needs, your closing ratio can reach as high as 90 percent. So, versatility is presenting the right products to the right people at the right time.

The phone has been the mainstay of my coaching practice for forty years. It's my go-to platform. But with the advent of fast and stable video, I have tried to motivate all my clients to talk on a virtual video platform. Not everybody is willing to connect their camera. Not everybody is proficient or confident enough to make the technology work. But for those I can talk to using video, my closing ratio has increased at least 30 percent. And yours will too.

Early in my career, I tried to visit prospects local to a speech I was presenting. One time the reverse happened. A prospect actually flew from Boston to Tampa to see me. It was closer than my home in California. We were scheduled to talk about his upcoming convention. I guess he thought that it was a good excuse to take that short vacation in a warm climate. But whenever I'm able to see a prospect face-to-face, my closing ratio rises to nearly 100 percent.

Video platforms have the same potential. There is so much more engagement from video versus the phone and so much more rapport and trust you can engender. Your closing ratio will increase dramatically as well.

Being versatile also means using the virtual video environment as more than just an extension of an audio platform. You are using many of the aspects that video media can provide. If you are meeting with somebody in person, you might have a written agenda. You might bring along a brochure outlining your services. When I meet with somebody face-to-face, I not only bring a brochure and written agenda to the meeting, I also bring one of my books I think could be relevant. Why would I do any less in a virtual video meeting?

While I can't bring a hard copy of a book to a video meeting, I can send an ebook to the client ahead of time. I can do a Slide-Share file of the meeting agenda the prospect can see on screen (PowerPoint is another platform to share a slide deck). I can also have testimonials included in the slide deck just in case I want to reference it. The only downside to a virtual meeting is not being there. Everything else can be nearly the same.

One big mistake many sales pros make is to email a handout to a prospect ahead of time. This is like giving the price to a prospect without attaching any value. As soon as they get the attachment, they will scroll to the last page and see the cost. That will bias everything else you say. There is no probing. They can't establish value. There are no benefits presented. All they read and think about is cost. Big mistake.

The correct way to show graphics during a virtual call is make it a part of the virtual SlideShare deck. You not only can control the flow of the meeting, but also select any slide at will while presenting. Let's say there is a question. You can type in the slide number and immediately pull it up. What if the prospect asks what the price is before you are ready? Since you are controlling the graphics, you are able to reveal the price at the appropriate time.

It is simple to say, "I don't know enough yet to answer that question. Can I get more information first?" Who is going to say no to that? They want you to gain enough information to meet their needs. They want to have an accurate price quote.

This scenario is even better than a face-to-face meeting. What if you arrived at the meeting and gave your prospect a folder of the presentation? Wouldn't they look at the first page and then turn to the last page looking for a price quote? In a virtual meeting, you can control everything the prospect sees, in the order they see it. You have total control. In fact, if the meeting ends too soon, your prospect will have to agree to schedule another to find out the cost. It's the best of all worlds.

Using Texts as Reminders

One negative of the virtual sale is getting people to show up. When I book a face-to-face meeting, I will send an email or text reminder the day before. I do the same for a voice phone call. But on a video platform call, I'm dependent on the prospect showing up on time. On a phone call, I can initiate the audio call without waiting. On a face-to-face meeting, I can also show up on time prompting the prospect to drop what they are doing to greet me. But virtual is different. There is a lot less pressure to show up on time. Many of my coaching clients are five to ten minutes late. That would never happen if I called them by phone or walked in their office.

Unless you are proactive in sending appointment reminders, there's a likelihood the prospect won't show up. It's important to make your meeting easy to attend. Prospects may be late because, at the last minute, they can't find the meeting reminder or lost the call-in phone and passcode. It's a huge waste of time. Your time. If you want to take out the friction, send a link to their email. They just have to click and join the meeting. Make it seamless and easy.

My assistant, Bethany, does the usual meeting reminder three days ahead and one day prior. If my client is a known tardiness offender, she will text ten minutes ahead of each coaching call. That usually does the trick. But the bottom line is you have to be a lot more protective of your time using a virtual platform than you would face-to-face or on the phone.

How Are We Doing on Time?

As I've mentioned earlier, not only is it important to guard your time, it is also critical that your prospect allocates enough time as well. You should let them know ahead how long the meeting will take. There is no guarantee they will remember, but at least there is a chance they will be prepared.

One of my clients is a branch manager for a large life insurance company. While a master salesperson, he also built a successful sales team. I learned from him to always check for time limitations at the beginning of any virtual meeting. After a few minutes of chatting, he will ask, "How are we doing on time?" He never wants a prospect to end the meeting prematurely. If the prospect does have time constraints, then he will be able to shorten the meeting and schedule a follow-up.

Think about how powerful this is. If you planned a one-hour meeting and the prospect says they only have twenty minutes, would you rush to the close or would you probe for needs and then schedule a follow-up? Would you push the presentation ahead or would you realize that the prospect probably won't say yes until you have enough time to present?

When you are prospecting for new business, don't ask how much time they have. A cold call, for example, is an interruption. If you ask about time, they will simply provide an excuse to get off the phone. But if you have a scheduled call, you don't want to be blindsided with an abbreviated time frame. In my audiobook *Tele-Sales: How to Get Business on the Telephone*, one of the concepts I talk about is fear of intrusion. This is displayed by telemarketers getting a prospect on the phone and then saying, "Have you got a minute?" This gives the prospect an immediate excuse to say they are busy and get off the phone.

One of the benefits of most virtual platforms like Zoom, Teams, Join.Me, and Webex is the built-in calendar. Once someone accepts your virtual meeting, simply add their email address to the appointment scheduler. The platform then reminds the participant three days prior and one day ahead of the event. This is a real time-saver in case you don't have an assistant available. You still might have to text the flagrant offenders a day ahead and ten minutes before the meeting to make sure they show.

I'm a big proponent of not wasting time dialing for dollars. If I connect with a referred lead and think they are worth talking to again, I don't want to dial another five times to get them back on the phone. I don't want the prospect to call me back when ready. Your time is valuable. Don't let prospects or even clients waste it.

"When they are ready" never happens. I am obsessive about not wasting my time. Nearly all prospects say they will call back. That never happens. Possibly they have the best of intentions. But life gets in the way and whatever is urgent becomes more important.

My response is always, "I love to keep myself organized as I'm sure you do. When is a good time to follow up?" They usually say, "In a couple weeks." I then look at my calendar and suggest a future date in a few weeks as they suggested. For example, I will say, "A couple weeks from now is Thursday the thirteenth. Is that a good time for you? Great, how about 10:40 on the thirteenth. Does that work?" They always say yes. Then you won't have to chase them and waste time.

Once in a while the prospect will not commit to a follow-up appointment. They will say something like, "I don't know what my schedule will be in two weeks. Let me call you back." If that happens, suggest a temporary appointment to serve as a placeholder. For example, "How about we pencil in 10:40 on the thirteenth? If that doesn't work, just let me know."

If they still don't accept your suggestion, the prospect is not qualified and are only looking for an excuse to waste more of your time chasing them. Simply accept their offer to call you back and walk away. They never will. Don't worry. You won't lose the lead. Later, I will talk about the Three-Month Phone Call. This is a way to keep prospects on a virtual follow-up system. A lot of my coaching clients are afraid of losing business if they don't agree to let the prospect call back when they want. You won't lose the lead. But you also won't waste your time. Depending on a prospect to call back is a fool's errand.

Suggest Virtual Video, Default to Audio

Since virtual video calls are so much more effective than audio, it's a good idea to make virtual your go- to default platform. This means suggesting virtual on every follow-up. About 25 to 30 percent of your prospects will ask for audio. Possibly they are traveling, using a cell, or don't have fast internet speed. They will let you know. But your mindset needs to be, "When in doubt, use video." With the advent of 5G, even cell phone video is nearly flawless everywhere there is a signal.

Unless your prospect is driving, using video, even on a cell, is better than audio alone. Make that your standard. Make it your mindset. Ask everybody if they will talk to you via video on the next appointment. Just as your closing ratio on a face-to-face is better than audio, your closing ratio on video will be better as well.

Sometimes prospects feel a slight level of intimidation using video. This is normal. You have also felt some anxiety. Each subsequent call becomes easier and more comfortable. But your closing ratio will increase if you use video. When your prospect unthinkingly says they would rather use audio, it displays a reflex response. This is the response people voice without thinking. For example, you walk into a clothing store thinking you would like to buy a blue blazer. The associate asks you upon entering, "Can I help you?"

Your reflex response is, "No thanks, I'm just looking." You came in to buy a blazer, yet you told the person you were just looking. Why?

Nobel laureate Daniel Kahneman wrote the landmark book *Thinking, Fast and Slow.* Kahneman discussed System 1 and System 2 thinking. System 1 thoughts are responses that come out of your mouth without much cognition. System 2 thinking is when you take a moment to evaluate various responses in an attempt to be correct. For example, when someone asks if I mind traveling in my career, my System 1 response surfaces that I hate traveling. But when asked about whether I enjoy speaking in front of groups, I love it. Travel to do what I love is a necessary evil. I often get a lot done on airplanes. I make travel very productive. I read magazine articles, respond to emails, and do research for whatever book I'm writing.

Your response to a System 1 comment should never be to blindly accept the first words that come out of someone's mouth. If you accept a System 1 unthinking retort, you may be getting only reflex response emotion. But just by asking a follow-up question, you can cause someone to move into a System 2, more thought-out response.

For example, what should the clothing shop associate have said knowing what you know now about System 1 and System 2? They would have never allowed a response from your System 1. To prevent a reflex response, they would've said, "You look like someone who loves to dress well. I bet you are looking for a blazer, a shirt, or a pair of pants. Am I warm?" It is rare to encounter a salesperson who says more than, "Can I help you?" But those who are able to move others into System 2 are the most engaging. These are the pros who make sales. Those who allow others to only access unthinking System 1 create friction.

Pacing

A smart way to move people into System 2 is through pacing. This is the mechanism of moving people in a directional flow of conversation they are already going and metaphorically walking with them. If someone walks into a store, they are obviously looking for something to buy. If you ask anything besides that goal, you are causing friction. When someone walks in the store, you might say, "You look like someone who knows what they want. What are you looking for?" The shopper will smile and tell you.

You may not be a retail sales associate, but yet you still allow people to respond from System 1. You greet them on the telephone during a virtual call by saying, "How are you?" Have you ever at any point received a response other than, "I'm fine thank you. How are you?" This is an artifact of communication. It produces the same response every time you ask. So why do you say it?

During one experiment at UCSD in grad school, we would answer trite questions with a terrible System 2 answer to gauge whether the other person was listening. In answer to, "How are you?" we might say, Well, I just found out I have cancer with only three months to live. I have to leave school and my family has to pay back my $150K in loans. Other than that, I am fine." The student seemingly didn't hear the terrible news and instead said, "Good, I am fine too." They had asked "How are you" expecting a System 1 response. They answered with their own

System 1 response. People reflexively answer what they expect to hear.

Your goal should be to get people into System 2 immediately. Why not develop rapport at the beginning of the conversation? Why waste the first few minutes on an artifact of communication? For example, "Hi John, I was just thinking about you yesterday. I read that snow is headed your way. Did you get pelted?" This will move John into System 2 and develop rapport faster.

I have never used, and hope I won't ever use, communication artifacts. Our time is too precious. On a virtual call, I show up at least five minutes early and wait for my client's name and picture or phone number to pop up. As soon as I notice their video and audio is on, I mention how nice their suit is or refer to some trophy in their office. For example, "I didn't know you were a golfer. What did you get the trophy for behind your head?" That starts off a conversation creating rapport.

The prospect might comment how he birdied hole number 18 winning the round. We know that rapport helps generate trust. We also know that an artifact like, "How are you?" generates nothing. Your time is precious in the first few minutes of any virtual meeting. Use it well.

Contact: The First Four Minutes

One of the most influential behavioral thinkers of my time was Los Angeles psychiatrist Leonard Zunin. He wrote a remarkable book in the 1970s called *Contact: The First Four Minutes*. Dr. Zunin suggested we make more than 93 percent of lasting impressions about people in the first four minutes. This means that people also make decisions as to whether or not they like and trust you in the first four minutes.

You have probably heard, "There is no second chance for a first impression." That is partly true. We tend to make decisions whether we like people in the first few minutes. This is because of System 1 thinking. A communication artifact like, "How are you?" just wastes part of the first four minutes to make a positive lasting impression. The right way to make a long-term impression is to move people into System 2 as fast as you can. This means get them talking.

If you make cold calls, you don't have time to move people into System 2. You simply need to use their name, make an interest-generating statement, and then do your best to probe for more information.

For example, "John Smith? Hi, Mr. Smith, my name is Kerry Johnson. I'm from Johnson Financial and I'm calling to see if I can save you $100 per month in Medicare supplement expenses. What kind of Medicare do you have now?"

On the other hand, if you have an appointment with someone you know, it's critical that you move them into System 2 as quickly as possible. The best way to do that is to ask questions about their business, life, or—better yet—trophies and mementos you see around their office during a virtual video call.

For example, you might say, "Hi, John. Thanks for your time today. I just noticed while you were connecting that you have some pictures of Apache helicopters. Do you have some connection to helicopters?" I mention Apaches because I recently had a conversation with a medical doctor who was a flight surgeon. This is the way I was able to get her to System 2 quickly. Continue this for four minutes. At that point, bring up your agenda for the meeting and ask what they would also like to accomplish. This will generate a lot more rapport and trust than if you simply used a communication artifact only generating a System 1 reflex response.

Getting Overwhelmed with Virtual Meetings

A downside of the new virtual environment is the sheer saturation of this media. In a pre-COVID-19 world, it was typical to have a phone conference call in the office followed by a staff meeting later on. Then possibly lunch with colleagues. The afternoon might entail a video conference with colleagues across the country. But there would be a mix of events to keep the day interesting.

In a post-pandemic world, the daily hike might be from the bedroom to the shower, followed by a seat at your kitchen table. For the next ten hours, the only movement would be from video call to video call. This would tax anybody's attention. Not only is it monotonous, the drudgery also facilitates burnout.

It is likely you are busy communicating virtually from dawn till dusk with barely enough time to take restroom breaks. Part of organizing yourself in a virtual world is to build in rest breaks between every call. But it is also important to have the discipline to maintain those breaks.

Besides possessing the discipline to maintain a schedule you can adhere to, it's also important to stay on time. I have discussed earlier how important it is to state the agenda at the beginning of every call. Then let all other participants know how much time the call will entail. When you get close to the termination point of the call, you could announce a five-minute warning before ending. There's actually no reason why any call should go over time. You need to take responsibility for making sure calls stay on time. Or at least ask permission to continue.

One of my frequent calls during most days is to those who want to connect on social media, specifically LinkedIn. I am always on time. After announcing the agenda, I let the participant know when I have to leave. Once you announce a deadline, it's important to stick to it for the sake of your own mental stability. There is nothing worse than going over ten minutes on every call, then being late for the rest of the day.

The US is one of the few countries that respects timeliness. Germany and Switzerland are two others. The manager of my home in Southern Portugal is Scottish. We often joke about how we are both early to appointments even over a social coffee. He said Portuguese practice "mañana time." Their idea of on time is thirty minutes after the appointment was supposed to start. But my Scottish friend will leave after a ten-minute wait. If they want to reschedule, he will lay down the rules. It's effective. One is only late once with him.

Block Out One Hour a Day

Another way to avoid virtual sales burnout is to block time in the morning and afternoon for research. My coaching calls are scheduled from the top of the hour to half past. There is a ten-minute float until forty past the hour, just in case. I allocate ten minutes to write my notes from the previous call and email them to the client. That allows me a minimum of ten minutes to take a bathroom break, grab a snack, refill my coffee, or even respond to a family text. The point of being so organized is to prevent overload. I don't want to be late to a business call. But any schedule will keep you prepared for an important engagement later.

Allowing your day to be chockablock does a service to nobody. It makes you seem disorganized and much less effective. But maintaining an organized schedule, and staying disciplined with it, helps you get more done in a more relaxed way. Stay disciplined to your schedule to avoid burnout.

3

Virtual Sales Calls

L ike a face-to-face appointment, virtual calls need structure too. It's amazing how many sales pros just wing it. They feel that sheer force of personality is all they need. That might be good enough in a retail store, but inadequate for selling higher ticket items.

The Structure of the Call

Being organized builds confidence in your prospect or client that you are competent to do what you promise. Being disorganized builds friction and causes prospects to doubt. The feeling that you are disorganized may come from being late to a call, experiencing technical issues, or perhaps not verifying that the platform is set up effectively before the call. You might make the prospect wait while you adjust sound or microphone. There are some very funny car insurance commercials showing a couple fighting while the wife is on a virtual call. Interruptions can do damage to your credibility and rapport.

All this bears on your ability to create rapport and trust. A prospect's confidence in you is built over time with the little things, not just the big ones. I commit clients to a six-month contract to keep them engaged. There is nothing worse than a client leaving after two months due to a lack of their own self-discipline. I constantly tell candidates that coaching will not work if you don't show up, don't study for five minutes every day, and don't do the tasks you commit to. When a client leaves coaching after a few months, it's like they never engaged in coaching at all and reverted to previous behavior like a rubber band.

Many years ago, I was ten minutes late to a call and apologized to my client. He told me he wanted to stop coaching because of my tardiness. I apologized again and couldn't understand why he was so unreasonably strict. He said his son was autistic. His family had to stay strictly organized otherwise everything would fly out of control. This also applied to how he conducted business. There were too many degrees of unpredictability in his family. He did not need another from his business coach. I hated to lose a client, but understood why. I was never late to a client appointment again.

The Virtual Call Format

The format of every virtual sales call needs to include these steps:

1. RAPPORT

It's always a good idea to take a couple of minutes to develop rapport. Of course, those minutes could be talking about the weather. But you can be more creative than that. Discussing a mutual friend is one idea. Noticing something about the prospect or their environment is also good. But don't skip this step. Developing rapport is key to generating trust.

A problem with this part of the call is overdoing the initial rapport portion of the call. During some virtual webinars and events, the organizers talk about baseball or sports not relevant to the rest of the group. Or worse yet, the moderator or organizer will delay the start of the meeting for tardy participants. This is not only a waste of time for those who show up on time, but also causes participants to avoid arriving on time in the future. They simply think the meeting won't be on time so why should they? Aside from a webinar, a virtual call with more than two participants should start on time. If the third participant is late, they can be updated briefly when they join the call.

A more correct and appropriate way of developing rapport on a virtual one-on-one sales call is to take no more than ninety seconds to develop rapport. Unless your prospect or client changes the agenda, with your agreement, assume they want to stay on task.

2. AGENDA

If you really want to gain confidence in your ability to keep commitments, an agenda is an essential first step. Think of the number of meetings you've attended in the last few days where the organizer just launched into the talking points. Sure, you were able to gain the gist of the conversation. But wouldn't it have been better if they laid out an agenda in the beginning of the meeting? Better yet, wouldn't it also have been helpful if they sent a written agenda to you the day before?

3. RECAP

This is the psychotherapeutic model of sales. The recap is the best way possible of making people feel understood. I will talk about a formal five-step probing process later. But if it's a new relationship, don't pitch. Listen. If it's a follow-up meeting, recap the main points from your last discussion. Get agreement and ask if they would like to add anything. Again, you are establishing a degree of organization to the meeting that most people don't see and will build confidence in your competence to get things done.

4. TRIAL CLOSE

Trial closing is one of the best ways to gain commitment. It's one thing to have a discussion with no follow-up. Sometimes your colleague becomes too busy. Other times they lose interest. But once you trial-close, you are getting the prospect to commit.

For example, "The last time we spoke, you wanted to talk about the warranty, the timing of delivery, and training. Is that correct?

If we could focus on these things today, will that be the right way to go?"

Your prospect will either say yes or change the agenda. Either way, you will save time and become much more efficient during your call.

5. FOLLOW UP

This step is possibly the most important. Sending a follow-up note is critical if you want to get something done. But make sure it's short.

Thank them for their time and list three talking points numerically. At the end, remind them of the follow-up meeting. Why three? We know that people forget 70 percent of what is said within one day, and 90 percent after three days. We also know that one need generates a 36 percent chance of a sale. Two needs equal 56 percent. Three needs close 93 percent of business as long as the solutions are workable. Did you notice I did not say four or five needs? More than three has a diminishing chance of returns. If you mention five or six items you discussed during the call, the prospect may remember nothing. Stick to three. Here's an example of an effective follow-up note by email.

> Hi John,
>
> It was good to meet with you today regarding improving your CRM. We discussed three things.
>
> 1. Scaling the CRM to include 10,000 records.
> 2. Making sure all your current fields are included in the new CRM.

3. Scheduling one day of training for your branch.

I look forward to talking to you on the thirteenth at 9:00 a.m. to discuss a training time that fits your branch administrative folks.

Sincerely,

Kerry Johnson

Obviously, the bigger the sale, the more meetings you will have. But bigger, more complex sales still include human behavior. People can only remember 3+/-2 items. Any more than that would become confusing. Any less becomes not very urgent. So keep all your meetings short and sweet. Make sure they stay organized with a trial close at the end of the meeting to keep them committed. Then follow-up with a note memorializing the three main points you discussed. If you use this model on every call, your closing ratio will go up and you will waste less time.

Audio Distractions

Good audio on a virtual call is important. But it is also critical to avoid distractions. Anything that takes your prospect's focus away will lower your closing rate. Think of a face-to-face appointment. Would you whisper or talk in a normal voice? Would you hide part of your face with a manila folder or would you rather make eye contact? These illustrations seem ridiculous. But these examples happen when you communicate virtually.

The sound could be difficult to hear. The internet connection can be so slow that your lips don't sync with what you're saying.

Your face might be pixelated. The only trait that makes a virtual connection work is to mirror the face-to-face environment so well that it's close to being there. Anything that distracts will cause friction.

HOW DO YOU SOUND?

Here are a couple of tips that will make your virtual calls more effective. Depending on your computer's microphone, you might sound like you are on a cell phone speaker. That might be fine during a short conversation with your spouse or kids. But you would never depend on a scratchy Bluetooth car audio speaker to help you make a sale. So why would you risk your computer's audio connection? New personal computers are lightning fast. In fact, most graphics cards are video game quality now. There is very little lag. Even watching a movie is incredible with high definition. The problem is often not video, but rather that audio quality has not yet caught up.

My recommendation is to invest in a USB 3.0 desk microphone. You might be tempted to just buy a cheap one. Instead, buy a mic that comes with installation software. When I bought my Sennheiser headset, it automatically installed on my PC. The software was embedded in my hardware. The microphone is top-notch. The speakers are studio quality.

I also bought a cheap microphone on Amazon for $10. My computer didn't recognize it and simply used the built-in PC microphone instead. While $10 wasn't exactly a big investment, it was still wasted money. You can use your PC's speakers, but don't scrimp on the microphone. Your virtual prospect won't hear your speakers. But they could be distracted by your microphone. This is critical. I personally think the desk microphone used by the late CNN host, Larry King, was pretty classy. I never noticed King's suspenders. But I did notice how big the desk mic was and how good it sounded. It was probably a prop with sound produced by microphones around the desk, yet his iconic mic was a focal point of the interview. *Dirty Jobs* host Mike Rowe also uses a desk mic for every interview. It sounds sharp and is never distracting. Just buy one that installs on your PC. It will have better sound pickup.

Generally, it's important for any audio device to be recognized. First go to your computer's sound devices. Next, look for the name of the microphone and speakers you're currently using. If you don't see them in the list of devices, instruct your computer to search. Whatever platform you use, Zoom, Webex, or even GoToMeeting, the virtual platform will always search for drivers that are recognized by the operating system.

One of the reasons I spent so much money on sound devices is that my Windows laptop will always recognize the Sennheiser drivers. As a rule, if you don't see the microphone or headset in the list of platform drivers, the operating system will probably use the one provided by your computer and bypass any external microphone that you might use.

ECHO IS BAD

Generally, when audio is bad, it's because of the microphone, not your speakers. But if your room is echoey, that could also be distracting. Many media network guests speak in big rooms only using Apple EarPods. You can usually hear their voices bounce off the walls. The studio host often has impeccable sound quality, which makes the guest's earbuds sound terrible by comparison. An answer is to set up your virtual call in a smaller room. You can also put blankets in front of your microphone to soak up the echoes. Since your voice is carrying forward, something needs to absorb the sound waves.

When I'm recording an audiobook, the studio is always first-rate and professional. The walls have baffles distributing and directing any ambient sound away from the microphone. The walls actually absorb most of the sound that hits them. There is never an echo or reverberation. In studio, I wear a headset in addition to using a stand-alone microphone. The director will usually correct me through the headphone if I mispronounce a word.

While none of us have the resources of a recording studio for our virtual calls, we should try to get as close to this audio quality as possible.

ACOUSTIC PANELS

One of the best ways to produce perfect sound is using acoustic panels. These panels are really fabric dividers with cloth held up by a frame. They are available on Amazon. Just search for audio fabric dividers. Telemarketing offices have used panels for decades in an attempt to isolate salespeople from the noise of the rep next to them. You can put one panel in front with two on the sides. This should not only protect you from background noise, but also prevent reverberation off the walls.

The right way to position these dividers is at each side of the computer and microphone. Any sound that rises won't echo as much as the sound that reverberates off the walls of your space. Don't put the dividers behind you or the video shot will look like you are in a prison cell. But depending on what is in front of your computer, such as a street or open window, you might want to put one of these dividers in front of your computer also.

If you don't want to use panels, blankets will work also. Just make sure they are thick. The bigger they are, the more noise they will absorb. Sheets will not work. Like the fabric dividers, don't allow blankets to be visible to your virtual call participant.

BACKGROUND NOISE

Some background noise is inevitable. You are likely to have some noise from traffic, office phones ringing, or even soft music. But when any ambient noise is consistent, it will be distracting. Friction will result.

I like soft jazz playing while I'm working. I think it's a mood changer, always putting me in a good frame of mind. But if I'm on a virtual call, any music in my room will get turned off. I don't want any distractions. What if my prospect doesn't like jazz?

Do you have a dog in your house? Are your kids playing loudly? Do delivery drivers ring the doorbell? All of these noises are hallmarks of at-home, remote, virtual calls. While a stray sound maybe totally acceptable, your goal should be to minimize all of these distractions. If your dog barks at every car that rolls down the street, perhaps put her in the spare bedroom during your calls. Maybe putting a sign on your door requesting that delivery drivers don't ring the doorbell can prevent some distractions.

While it's difficult to completely soundproof everything, it's important to get as close to a distraction-free call as possible. My home office is pretty darn quiet. My golden retriever, Sadie, is well-trained and never barks. My daughters are adults. I jokingly say they only call when they want money. Even my wife, Merita, respects my workday enough not to come in my home office when I'm on a call. During emergencies, she will put a note on my desk waiting for a thumbs-up or thumbs-down response. The only variable is the garbage truck that visits Thursday mornings. But even then, it is only noticed when I leave the door to my workspace open.

I don't need to say this, but I will. Turn off your telephone and cell phone ringers. The dings and rings are distracting and unprofessional.

Remote Locations

Recently, I was a panelist on a conference call with fifty attendees from all over the US. I told the organizer that I would be flying from Los Angeles and landing in Washington, DC, at 4:30 in the afternoon. I traveled to see my grandkids for the weekend. The call was scheduled for 5:30 p.m., so I felt safe that I wouldn't have to retreat to my backup plan of calling from the airport American Airlines Admirals Club. It was only fifteen minutes to my daughter's house. I logged on from the dining room. When I started, both kids were taking naps. The house was quiet.

After twenty minutes, my grandson, Lincoln, woke up and was unhappy. At four months old, his cries carried throughout the house. When my time came to participate, I noticed that I had been muted by the organizers. Every time I unmuted myself to make a comment, they would mute me again. This went on for about five minutes. Finally, they let me know how distracting my environment was. While I could hear Lincoln crying, I didn't realize how much the noise carried on the call. I needed a quieter place. I walked upstairs to a back bedroom. The internet was weaker in that part of the house, and I risked the call being dropped.

While I have a backup plan for my home office, I didn't have one for the remote location at my daughter's house. If I had been prepared, I would've tested the upstairs for the least amount of echo and the fastest internet available. The fact is I was unprepared. My grandson's crying left me with a poor-quality call and a lot of distractions.

During the pandemic when everybody worked from home, there was a lot of forgiveness of household noise. But when people trickled back to the office, there is now a much shorter amount of patience. Not only will your home need to be soundproofed with few distractions, it will need to be the same as the office environment. Even if you share an office with another, there is little tolerance for distractions.

I've spoken before about the use of earbuds and how poor the microphones are in them. While it's acceptable to use earbuds, make sure the microphone is wired directly to the USB connection in your computer. Better yet, use a boom mic mounted on your desk. Make sure it's six to eight inches away from your mouth. Regardless of which mic you use, try to select one that is noise canceling. This will minimize ambient noise no matter where you are. It will drown out heating and air conditioning noise. It will minimize ringing from your cell phone (which you need to mute anyway), and even drown out the odd garbage truck rumbling outside.

Desk mics are surprisingly inexpensive. You can get a good one for as low as $30. Noise-canceling mics are a little more money, but worth it. I use corded noise-canceling earbuds for airplane flights. It is surprising how good a noise canceling microphone is.

On most virtual platforms, you can separate the earbud from the microphone. For example, your virtual platform will identify a desktop mic as separate from an earbud. As an aside, make sure your microphone is great quality. This is far more important than the earbud. You need to sound as good as possible to your virtual call partner.

Lighting: The Big Challenge

Lighting during virtual video calls is nearly always bad. If there is any light at all, it usually comes from normal fixtures in the ceiling. Often celling lights aren't strong enough to illuminate your face. Sometimes sunlight comes in totally drowning out your face. Even in my home office, the morning sunlight cuts across my face, masking the video. Every office needs lighting consistency for video.

Over the last thirty years, I have created nearly one hundred business-building videos. Many recordings were done at the Herbalife Studios in Los Angeles. Most shoots were all-day affairs producing only one or two videos. There were two cameras with teleprompters. I wore a lavaliere microphone and had an overhead boom mic. The sound levels took a few minutes to prepare.

The camera distance and teleprompter set-up was not that tough. The real effort was in the lighting. Getting the lights right took hours and hours. While the studio technicians were pros, there's a big difference between them and other studios I have used. Spending an hour trying to get rid of a few shadows is common. But it's also the difference between an amateur and broadcast-quality production.

The quality of your virtual call doesn't have to be as high as if you're lighting a TV news anchor. But again, we are trying to diminish distractions. Anything that takes away from the content of your call will hurt your closing ratio. Any distraction will create friction.

An ideal lighting idea is to use inexpensive ring lights. They should face you but be positioned in back of the camera. These circular lights can be plugged into any wall socket. You need enough

Lighting behind your computer won't make you look as well lit as a TV anchor, but it's a sound technique for showing you in your best light.

light to illuminate your face, but not so much that you will be washed out.

Shannon Bream is the host of *Fox News @ Night*. She is also the legal expert on the Fox News Channel. In studio, she appears well lit, has an attractive background, and precise audio. But her remote set looks like it was shot at a studio at her house. There are bright spots on her forehead and cheeks inconsistent with the rest of her torso. She looks like an intern came to her house and set up a homemade lighting kit. While good enough for a virtual call, it is not the right quality for cable news.

During the pandemic, it was obvious which news reporters were set up in hotel rooms or bedrooms or makeshift sets on remote locations. Again, we were forgiving, but no longer.

Backdrops

The best backdrops reflect who you are. I always appreciate bookcases behind an intellectual who is being interviewed. I think it's appropriate to see sports trophies behind an athlete. I also think that an executive might be well served during a virtual call sitting in a company boardroom. It could even be appropriate for the CEO to have a logo of the company displayed behind their head. The bottom line is the background should reflect your brand.

One company I coach in the solar panel business has salespeople throughout Southern California. At times, they are in the Los Angeles office talking to me from a cubicle. Other times, they call in from homes. They frequently will hide, speaking from their kitchen or bedroom by using a virtual backdrop provided by the platform. For example, Zoom has many virtual backdrops you can use. The problem is the backdrops are inconsistent with who these people are. When is an image of the Taj Mahal in India appropriate when you are a solar salesperson?

Another backdrop is the redwoods in Northern California. Unless you have a green screen background on which to superimpose an image, stock Zoom backdrops never look flattering. They also rarely mirror your brand. Stock backdrops can also be distracting. When the user turns their head, sometimes an ear is missing. The worst of these backdrops cause half of the user's face to disappear. It is better not to use any stock platform background generated electronically. Unless you can use a green screen, it will only distract from the content of the call.

Some of the best backgrounds I've seen are on TV with a company logo displayed. It is actually easy to copy an image and expand it on a video screen. You can use a PowerPoint image to display it or even use Microsoft Word to paste the logo in the document and project it on a screen behind you.

If you can afford a background image you want, be sure to use one that communicates what you do and who you are. I spent a lot of money creating a dark wood library for my video recordings. While it is full of books, my own writings are prominent in the frame. Usually, my newest book is front and center among all the others. I want my virtual call participants to ask about my books. In fact most authors will have their book(s) displayed prominently in the frame of every call. If you can't spend $10,000 building a library in your home office, at least you can spend some money on a trade show booth type of image to put behind your chair.

These booths can be as small as four feet standing on a table or a six-foot version you see at most trade shows. As a side benefit, most of us use our trade show booths a few times a year and then park them in a storage area. But you have a new use for a booth utilizing it daily during your calls.

Think about it. Would you go to a convention and sit in an empty booth? Or would you dress it up with images surrounded by products and promotional materials related to what you do? A virtual background image should be viewed the same as a trade show. You want to control what the prospect or client sees. But above all, it needs to be consistent with the purpose of the call.

Filters

The use of any kind of filter can be distracting. They are a lot of fun on iPhones. Teens use them frequently to distort faces or add bunny ears to people's pictures. But if you include them in your business, you will terminally kill any credibility you might have on a virtual call.

This is a good reminder to test your virtual call settings. Have you heard of Murphy's Law? "Anything that can go wrong will go wrong." I believe in O'Toole's Law, "Murphy was an optimist. If there is a worst time for something to go wrong, it will happen then." What all this means is that you need to test your settings and run through your call before it happens. Especially if you are doing a demo or webinar, O'Toole will reign.

I recently did a webinar on The Virtual Sale to more than one hundred attendees on my least favorite platform, GoToWebinar. It isn't as user-friendly as some others or easier to mute yourself and others. The organizer who worked hard to market the meeting did a ten-minute intro about his company before he introduced me. Unfortunately, he only got in three minutes of the ten, then dead silence. I thought the meeting was disconnected and muted and unmuted myself several times before I realized it was just him.

When you think you are totally prepared for the meeting, go through it five more times. You don't want to be embarrassed and waste your hard work putting it all together.

Other Distractions to Avoid

Here are some backdrops to avoid in your camera shot.

CLUTTER OR RUBBISH.

It's fairly easy to empty the trash basket on the floor. It may not be so obvious to fold a blanket or straighten up wiring or cables. This could also be distracting to the viewer. Anything they can see in your screenshot that may cause them to avert attention from you and your agenda is unhelpful.

BLANK WALLS.

It may seem that blank walls are the perfect backdrop. After all, real estate agents often say the best house to show has neutral colors. But that is not the case with virtual video. White or beige

Avoid distractions in your background such as clutter, blank walls, lighting that washes you out or puts you in the dark, or distracting items.

walls only make your environment look like a prison. If you must show a blank room, at least limit what the viewer sees. Position the camera so that it displays only one wall. You may even want to put your chair in a corner of the room and minimize the size of the camera's frame. This is often seen in mainstream media interviews. The guest is in a corner with a limited view of two walls.

BRIGHT LIGHT SHINING THROUGH WINDOWS.

It could be a good idea to cut up some cardboard and tape it to the inside of the offending windows. It's never enough to only cover up the distracting sunlight you see before the call. It's better to predict where the sun will shine thirty minutes into the call. You don't want to interrupt the phone call so that you can cover a window or pull a shade. You especially don't want a prospect or client to stop the meeting because they can't see you.

DISTRACTING ART AND DECORATIONS.

A picture of four dogs playing poker on velvet is bad enough. But when your eclectic taste in art is reflected in the background of your virtual video frame, it may cause enough distraction that your prospect makes a comment. It's always been said that the frame of a painting should accentuate the painting itself. The frame should never be noticed. That is what you're going for in a virtual video background shot. You don't want the viewer to notice the pictures. You don't want the viewer to pay attention to anything except you.

A BIG ROOM OR HALL.

The bigger the room you conduct the virtual video call from, the more distracting it will be. It's important to limit the view of the prospect or client. Think of it this way. Assume you have friends over for a party in the living room. After a conversation, you want to show off the reclining chair. As you walk into the cavernous room, they walk by some artwork on one wall and a statue on another. They stop to notice a few bottles of scotch at the wet bar. They peruse books piled up in a corner, finally noticing the reclining chair you're so proud of.

This is exactly what your virtual video call viewer will do. Even though you start the call saying hello and making eye contact, they notice every aspect of your space sequentially. They are unlikely to pay attention to you until they can inspect what is behind you. They become distracted and unable to listen to anything you say in the first few minutes. Do you really want that to happen? Wouldn't you instead like to gain rapport and get down to business with their full attention?

One of my favorite backgrounds is a simple bookcase. You can pick one up at IKEA for less than $100. It will take you about an hour to assemble (good luck). After that, you can fill it with all your books and magazines. The bookcase can be positioned behind and even frame the books around your head. This is a simple way to produce a neutral backdrop your prospect or client will not be distracted by.

After graduate school, I was so attracted to libraries that I went to garage sales and picked up books with attractive covers just to put in my bookcases. Some of these books were of little interest. But I wanted my library to look full. In time, as I bought books I wanted to read, I got rid of the fillers and replaced them with the ones I wanted.

Anytime I had a house party and gave friends a tour of my library, they would always ask, "Have you read all these?" It was always super embarrassing to say no. But after forty years, I can honestly say that I've read at least part of every book in my library. Even today during a virtual video call, prospects and clients will ask if I've read all the books they see in the video frame. I'm especially proud when they look at my library and ask which ones I wrote. I will usually stand up and grab two or three, showing prospects my most current projects. It's a perfect icebreaker and rapport developer.

What Room Is Best?

Have you ever noticed how someone's house is decorated while they are being interviewed during a broadcast? Sometimes they are in a kitchen. Other times, it's a family room. Regardless, it's hard not to look at how the room is decorated or even notice the color of their bedspread. Have you ever been distracted looking at their pillows on a couch? Or glimpse an unmade bed? A cat strolling through. The vase of flowers. It almost seems as though someone is lurking around their room? It takes a while to calibrate, doesn't it? It's almost as if you are watching a TV reporter on the street who doesn't seem to notice a drunk. The viewers notice. The camera operator hopes the drunk will stay away. But the reporter keeps going not knowing what is behind the shot. While not this severe, you still have to minimize distractions in your shot.

Most of the time, you will be speaking to a virtual video amateur using a home set-up. They likely focus only on whether the computer is plugged in and turned on. Little else is of concern. Lighting and sound are secondary considerations. Poor lighting and poor-quality sound are one thing. Background, walls, colors, and furniture are distant considerations.

But all of these create friction and take away from your message and content. You have to do a lot more to keep attention on video. It's always amazing to me to see a Fortune 500 CEO with a dirty kitchen. You expect wealthy people to control their environment better. In one interview, I saw a fish mounted on a plaque behind the speaker's head. It took a few minutes to focus on what he was saying. I kept wondering if the fish might start singing.

On Fox News *The Journal Editorial Report*, some reporters speak via video from their living rooms. It is always distracting. The show airs on Saturdays, so one thinks the guests are home with family. But it almost feels as if you are in their living room, uninvited and lurking. You feel slightly embarrassed for the person you are eavesdropping on. It has the impression of looking in their medicine cabinet.

The answer to all this is to minimize what the viewer can see. You want them to see a small space instead of a big one. You want them to see a corner instead of a big living room. You want them to see books, mementos, and awards instead of blank walls. In short, you want them to see a staged image instead of what you look like when you get home from work. It's worth staging your background as much as you maximize the sound quality and video image.

Framing

Perhaps the most frequent mistake virtual video users make is wrongly framing the picture. Often participants either don't notice how they look on screen or don't care. I'm sure you've seen people on video calls who never look at the camera. Or there is so much empty space above their head that you pay more attention to the ceiling than to their eyes. All of these distractions cause friction during the call.

One of the worst video images is the person who seems cut off because the camera is positioned too low. We are in an era of 24/7 cable news and interview channels. Professional newscasters use the camera effectively. Of course, they have directors who are able to adjust the camera angle at any time. While you don't have a director supervising your shots, you can control the frame of what the client or prospect sees. See the diagram showing the angle and spacing where your head should fit in this template.

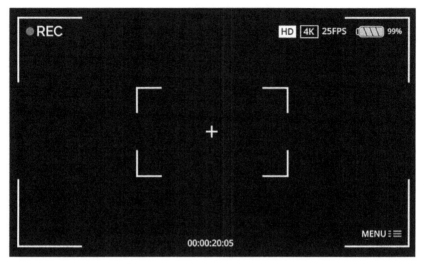

REC   HD 4K 25FPS 99%

+

00:00:20:05   MENU

Your head should be framed in the bracketed middle.

A good rule of thumb is to make sure the camera lens is the same height as your eyes. If you have a laptop on your desk, you will be tempted to look down at the camera. Even if you adjust a low camera higher to prevent empty space above your head, you may be producing a Keystone effect. This distortion will create an elongation of your face. It will also take attention away from you.

If you want to use a laptop camera, buy a six-inch-tall stand. This way the internal camera mounted on top of your laptop screen will be the same height as your eyes. Even better is to buy a high-quality USB camera with a stand positioning the lens at eye height. This way you never have to adjust the angle. It will always be perfect. If you have a laptop that is less than one year old, the camera is likely good enough quality to be passable. But a stock computer camera will last only a few years.

Proper video framing is as important as the sound or background. In fact, more so. You are competing against a high bar set by broadcast media. While you don't have a director and a studio, you can get as close as possible to high quality. Your goal is to avoid distractions.

Here are a few examples of what not to do. You have seen these mistakes. In fact, if you use virtual video frequently, you rarely see examples of proper framing. Most are terrible. See if you can tally the following mistakes you see most.

In group settings, it's easy to see attendees who are improperly framed with camera angles too high or too low.

THE SIDE SHIFTER

This video framing mistake is born of an improperly situated camera. Normally, even cameras that come stock with a laptop are positioned at the top of the screen. But sometimes, the virtual participant looks down to the side away from the camera. Possibly study notes rest on the side of the computer. It may also be that the prospect is checking a cell phone for messages. Regardless, it is distracting.

One of my clients is a side shifter. He may look directly at me during the first part of the call, but that's it. The rest of the video call shows him looking to the side of the camera. It is hard for me to stay focused. I don't mind someone taking notes during the call. I also don't mind if they divert their eyes to read something for reference. But it's important to maintain eye contact as much as you can. I constantly get the feeling that I'm losing my client's attention. Their focus is somewhere else. I find myself trying to reengage them using tie-downs. I will ask, "What are your thoughts?" too often. I don't feel that I've kept their attention and try too hard to reconnect with them.

Before COVID-19, a remote broadcast TV interview would be a camera facing a guest with a microphone on their lapel and an earbud. The viewer could see the host and the guest. The host had a video monitor. But the guest, unless they were in the studio, could never see anything. They were usually told to look at the camera.

This is distracting since the guest could hear, but not see. This is what it feels like talking to a side shifter.

CEILING ENVY

This one is common. The camera is positioned showing the virtual caller looking down. We often get a good view of the ceiling, and can even see the crown molding. But it is distracting as we try to make eye contact. Often room lights are in the ceiling. Regardless, the attention isn't on the prospect or client. Since the camera is pointed up, there is also severe facial washout, which only adds to the distraction.

THE POTATO HEAD

The Potato Head is another view you might see frequently. Their face fills up the whole frame. While also producing a Keystone effect for distortion, this view is super distracting, not allowing the viewer to see any background at all. Only their face. The skin tones may be off since the face is so close to the camera. Most good cameras are effective at registering skin tones. But not when they are inches away from the camera. The nose is front and center and any wrinkles are pronounced.

In the 1980s, Dustin Hoffman played the lead role of a male impersonating a female newscaster. He was trying to make it into broadcast TV and women were more sought after than men. In the movie *Tootsie*, the floor stage manager was told to back the actor away from the camera. The manager asked, "How far?" The director said, "How about Cleveland." This is the way people feel when you get too close to the camera. They don't know how to tell you to back up, you just have to know to do it.

THE ASTRONOMER

The astronomer frame is also poor framing. This is displayed by a head looking up at the camera. Your view is of the top of the caller's head looking down. Not only can you see the top of their head, you can actually see what's in the wastebasket next to them. This supplication

posture is never a good idea even if you don't believe in the psychology of communication. It almost has the image of an orphan looking up at the headmaster asking for more food in a Charles Dickens novel.

MR. ANONYMOUS

This is less frequent but equally bad. I have spoken a lot about lighting and how to position external lights behind the camera. You should use a ring light facing you. Ceiling lights are always a good idea as long as you have at least one light facing you. Most new cameras will magnify available light. But Mr. Anonymous has no light illuminating his face. It's almost as if *60 Minutes* was trying to protect a foreign spy from being recognized. Never allow light to shine behind you unless there is even more light shining at your face from the front.

THE EMPTY HEAD SPACE

This frame is common since the camera shows twice as much space above the head as below. Most people who show space above make the mistake of setting up the camera without previewing the frame. A quick fix is

angling the camera down a little. But a better solution is to make sure the camera is the same height as your eyes. While being easy to correct, few people notice the empty frame and how distracting it can be.

THUNDER FINGERS

This is a rare framing mistake, but still equally distracting. The camera is positioned far away from the face. When the subject is typing, all the viewer sees are huge imposing fingers tapping away. Perhaps a mouse is being clicked or your prospect is tapping away at the keyboard while taking notes. Either way, if your fingers are in the picture frame, the other caller is not looking at you. Anything is bad that distracts or takes away from your ability to generate rapport and trust. The prospect or client should never be able to see your fingers. Unless you want to use your hands to gesture. Generally, you should save your fingers and gestures for the time you want to accentuate a point.

A poorly positioned camera angle. Prospects should never see your fingers in the frame unless you are gesturing.

THE CORRECT FRAME

We all make framing mistakes on every call. Some show the top of a head while others show the desk below. No matter if you are on a Zoom call or participating on a broadcast panel, the frame of the shot needs to be correct. If your framing is distracting, you will lose attention.

Make the top of the frame two inches above your head. If the viewer can see anything above your head, it will take attention away. It is also appropriate to show your torso down to mid chest level. Any more of your torso will move attention away from your face. It is tough enough to read body language. The caller needs to be able to see your face clearly.

The side of the frame is also important. Two inches on the side is good. But since your frame will be rectangular, the shot can have more space on the side than at the top edge to your head. Most of

Correct framing, even lighting, out-of-focus background, a perfect image for a virtual call.

us move when we talk. We usually sway sideways but not up and down. Unless you are a three-year-old, you probably won't jump up and down during a call. For that reason, space on the side is a good buffer. Some cell phone shots don't have a rectangular space. But no matter what camera you use, still try to keep two inches above your head as a general rule.

The way to correct all of these framing mistakes is to log on a few minutes ahead where you can see your shot on the computer screen. Pay special attention to how your face is framed. What does the room behind you look like? Do you notice the face in the frame or the distractions from behind? Do you notice anything in the background? Could anything in the room take away from your prospect or client's focus on you? If so, move them. Close doors and adjust blinds. These are all important aspects to consider as you sell virtually.

One of my clients uses a brilliant strategy in meeting new prospects in his office. He greets them and chats when they walk in. He leads them to his office and asks if they want something to drink. Often, they say no, but he leaves anyway to get himself something. The ritual isn't to get a drink. It's to leave the prospects alone long enough to adapt to their surroundings. Above the desk is a TV playing a conservative business channel. The walls have pictures of his kids including some military service photos from his Army days. There are golf photos and pictures of past vacations. When he walks back in, visitors are acclimated and often say, "Who waters all these plants?" They chat about the types of plants and get down to gaining rapport and start the agenda. All this is done to limit distractions during the meeting.

You should treat the beginning of every virtual meeting with the same care. You can control the environment when a prospect comes to your office. You probably will take some time to organize and clean it up. You can also control your attention when meeting in a prospect's disorganized and unruly office.

I was in a branch manager's office many years ago. Papers were piled nearly to the ceiling. There were full ashtrays everywhere. It smelled like a smokestack. I even had to step over clothes on the floor to sit in a chair. But I could still control my own attention. You can't depend on your prospect or client exerting the same control during a virtual call with your own office or home as a background.

The setting has to be perfect. You have to give yourself the best chance of developing rapport and trust. Make sure your agenda is followed and your solutions are memorable. When using a phone, all you have to worry about is the sound quality. You are able to focus on the sales process by employing good listening techniques that helps you gain rapport.

But on a video call, not only do you have to ensure the sound and video quality are good, you have to do much more. Video communication is a new skill set that you must master if you want to be successful in this new sales environment. Virtual calls will never go away. If anything, more and more of your prospects and clients will ask to use video. The virtual sales platform won't end when a pandemic is under control. This medium will be with us for the long term.

As we discussed earlier, big ticket sales will be reserved for face-to-face meetings. Conferences will still be held in person.

Sales conferences will return because of their efficiency to generate leads. But all the discussions before and after a big sale will be virtual. Virtual video should not be intimidating. But you need to study and practice. It's a new skill set that will require proficiency.

Currently only a few training programs present information on how to conduct a successful virtual sale. The process is too new. But from books like this, you will gain the information you need to become proficient. All you have to do is practice. Above all, take notes when you see people doing virtual video calls poorly. You probably engage in virtual calls many hours during every day. You have lots of chances to practice. Notice the calls that set the stage to help you feel comfortable and stay focused. Also pay attention to the calls in which you have the greatest rapport. How are the faces framed? What kind of backgrounds do you see? How is the camera positioned? What kind of microphone are they using? What kind of mic sounds better and which are worse?

In no time, you'll see best practices. From the examples presented here, you will be able to see the best way to structure and create virtual calls. I want to give you the best chance to create success and close more sales. The rest is up to you.

Dress for Success

I am often asked how you should dress during a virtual video call. I have seen callers wear everything from pajamas to a nice dress shirt with jean shorts. I have seen the range of attire from white T-shirts to tank tops. It seems as though the virtual call is a new free-for-all forum and few have any decorum. Would you dress randomly in a client's office? Would you ignore dress codes if you were about to see a new prospect in your office?

The answer is to dress as you would face-to-face. Would you go into an office wearing workout clothes? Would you visit a corporate executive in tennis shorts or yoga pants? Then why would you wear anything but professional attire on a video call? This is not the time to be overly relaxed and unthinking about how you look. This is also not the time to downplay the importance of what a client sees. On an audio phone call, you can dress however you want. But for some reason, perhaps because of the novelty of video, we seem to think that people no longer notice how you dress.

During a recent CBS news show, the reporter sat behind his desk speaking to the show anchor. The reporter had a coat and tie on and looked sharp. Unfortunately, below the desk, he was wearing only underwear. He didn't even have socks or shoes on. As soon as he signed out and the anchor thanked him for the report, the reporter stood up showing a million viewers whether he had boxers or briefs. I guess video delay is only available on some shows.

Even my favorite weekly hard news show, *Special Report* on Fox News, has its fair share of dress faux pas. Bret Baier, the host, was doing the 2020 presidential election coverage with Martha Mac-Callum. As the camera panned out for a commercial break, viewers were able to see a very dapper, Brooks Brothers–suited Bret Baier wearing white socks and tennis shoes as an accessory. I'm sure he felt the camera never panned out during his daily news show. But they were using a new set for election coverage that showed a lot more. The camera exposed the anchor's choice in sneakers. While seemingly harmless, would you wear a nice suit and tennis shoes to your prospect's office?

While all this is humorous and has no impact on your life except as a conversation piece, having a wardrobe malfunction on one of your virtual video calls could be embarrassing if not disastrous. What if your prospect had a suit on while you wore a T-shirt? What if you were on your way to play tennis after the video call dressed in tennis attire and your prospect just came out of a boardroom meeting? Would it make a difference? Yes, because the distraction will take at least a few minutes for the prospect to recalibrate and listen to what you have to say.

The 1/2 Dress Up Rule

Here is a basic rule: Always dress on a virtual video call at least one-half level above what you think your prospect will dress. If you think they will be in a polo shirt, men should wear a sports coat. If you think your male prospect will wear a dress shirt, men might put on a tie and jacket and women should have a dressy blouse (not sleeveless) and pearls or tasteful necklace. You can always take your jacket off. But if you have on a polo shirt and the prospect has a shirt and tie, it will be awkward for you to leave the room to put on more appropriate attire.

Does the way you dress really impact your prospect or client's level of rapport on a virtual video call? Yes, it does. Especially if it's an important meeting. The movie *Evita* has been remade several times. The last version featured Madonna in the starring role. It is about the life of Argentine dictator Juan Perón and his wife, Eva.

This is risky to dress only from the waist up.

In the prelude to World War II, Perón was second in succession to the presidency. Unfortunately, the then-current president became jealous and jailed Perón for a contrived corruption charge. His wife, Eva, led rallies in an attempt to free her husband. Finally, after his release from prison, Eva, nicknamed Evita as a term of endearment, organized a huge rally of union workers. During the event, Perón made a speech on the scaffolding high above the crowd. As he started his address, Evita took his jacket off and folded it in her arms. Taking the cue, Perón rolled up his sleeves and took his tie off. When the crowd saw that Perón was one of them, they cheered wildly adding momentum to his quest to take over the presidency and the government.

Perón was among the most consequential presidents of Argentina. His followers, ninety years later, are still called Peronists. Did his ascendancy happen because he took his jacket off? Probably not. But the voters felt Perón was one of them.

This is the type of emotion you want to convey on a virtual video call. You are an expert, which is communicated partly by the way you dress. But you are also willing to take your jacket off, roll up your sleeves, and get to work with your client. This is the image and emotion that help create sales. All of my coaching clients use the 1/2 dress up rule in meeting new prospects and existing clients. All of them want to gain rapport as quickly as possible. But they also know it's a lot easier to dress down than to make the mistake of not dressing well enough.

Many years ago, a meeting planner made the mistake of writing business casual on my speaker contract instead of business dress. When I arrived at the meeting in Las Vegas, I noticed all the attendees wearing suits and ties. Thankfully, I arrived an hour early. I didn't have a dress shirt or a tie. But I was wearing a sports coat. I walked to the atrium in the middle of the casino and spotted a gift store, not yet open. I persuaded the clerk to let me in and asked if they sold shirts. I was lucky enough to buy an overpriced shirt and tie saving me from being dressed inappropriately for the speech.

The biggest dress mistake I ever made was on my honeymoon. Before the time of COVID-19 and virtual video calls, my wife, Merita, and I were on our way to board a plane to Hawaii. On December 23, after our wedding the day before, we were scheduled to fly from Los Angeles to Honolulu for a seven-day cruise. Merita is a flight attendant with American Airlines. Flight attendants and their families can fly non-revenue (free) when there is space available. Flying stand-by is always nerve-racking. You never really know if you are going to make the flight.

Not only did the airplane have seats available, there were luckily two open in first class, which almost never happens. The gate agent told me they were ours if I had a tie. Unlike today, first class thirty years ago had a dress code. He didn't mention a dress shirt, so I figured all I had to do was find a store with a tie. I ran down the concourse desperately looking for a tie. Back in those days, security was minimal and only included a magnetometer checking for guns and knives. They didn't even verify boarding passes. You could actually walk briskly through the whole screening process.

After running through the concourse and checking three stores with no luck, and with only ten minutes before departure, I was getting desperate. Outside the terminal, I saw a religious cult member begging for money. These cult members had shaved heads and dirty street clothes only worn when begging for money at airports. With post-9/11 security, they can no longer walk past TSA, limiting their activities. But the one I met had a tie on.

He asked for a donation. I asked how much he wanted for the tie. Looking down, he said, "This old tie?"

I said, "I will give you $20 for that tie."

He said, "It's not worth $20."

I wasn't used to negotiating down in price but still countered my offer and said, "Okay, I will give you $10 for the tie."

He took it off and I gave him the $10. I ran to the gate with three minutes to spare. I put the dirty tie on under the collar of a polo shirt. The gate agent smiled at the combination. He took pity on me and said, "I didn't think you would make it." He gave us the first-class tickets. After boarding, I threw the tie in the trash and realized how lucky I was to be able to spend $10 for first class. I even got some exercise sprinting through the terminal. That would never happen today.

Airport rules are quite different now, and you can sit in first class wearing a bathing suit with a mask. But there is a lesson here. Always dress one-half level better than what you think the prospect and client will. You don't want any distractions and there is no second chance to make a first impression.

Internet Connections: How Fast Is Fast?

Have you ever noticed someone on a video call who looks pixilated? Or worse, their mouth doesn't match the words coming out? Slow internet speed can cause this and other big problems. It is less common these days to have an internet connection less than 1 Mbps. Perhaps rural areas with spotty satellite connections are the exception, but most populations, even in small towns, have fast internet available.

Twenty years ago, I called AT&T complaining about dropped calls. They responded with the excuse that cell phone coverage was not perfect. But now it is. Can you remember the last time you had a dropped call? There are few instances where I need to warn my caller about the possibility of bad reception.

Internet stability is even better in your home. Ten years ago, a fast internet speed would be 10 to 20 Mbps. Today, most cable operators can provide over 350 Mbps for about $100 a month. This is one of the reasons many of us are cable TV cord cutters, opting for video streaming at about 30 percent of the cost.

In fact, your cable company is likely to provide the fastest internet available while you work at home. Even if you don't get expense reimbursement from your company, fast internet is still a great personal investment. It's not whether you have fast internet, it's whether you are willing to risk a connection glitch. You don't need that headache.

Obviously, you want to make calls from your home office as close to the router as possible. But even in a large house, internet extenders can make any room as fast as the one closest to the router. Some of these extenders, called mesh networks, produce extremely high speeds even in a 10,000-square-foot house.

Here are a few tips to make sure your virtual video connections operate as smoothly as possible.

Make sure you get a tri-band router. This is a fast 5G router that can downshift to 2.4G if necessary. While 5G is faster, 2.4G extends farther. Most video platforms like Zoom are seamless with 2.4G. Generally, you don't want to risk a slower speed on an important call. The reason a tri-band router is important is that the signal will cycle from 5G to the next high-speed connection (5G2) to the last 2.4G connection if the 5G connection is lost. All of this will be seamless and should have no impact on the quality of your video call. You will have even less impact on an audio-only call using Voice over Internet Protocol (VoIP).

Upload speed is more important than download. It's really important in watching streaming movies to have a very fast download speed. In fact, the faster the better. Theoretically, each high-definition movie requires about 10 Mbps. So, with a 50 Mbps download speed, you could actually watch one movie and download four others for future viewing. But upload speed is what matters with virtual calls. This is the audio and video your caller hears and sees. When the speed is slow, your voice will not match your mouth.

The rule of thumb is to get the upload speed to 10 Mbps. You could probably get away with 3 Mbps if necessary. But internet speed is always variable. With a cable modem, you're sharing bandwidth with all your neighbors using the same service. At my home in California, Cox internet has a box on the property line next to my house. But that box distributes the signal to at least five other houses. If all my neighbors are using video at the same time, my speed will decrease greatly.

I have a VoIP telephone provided by Cox also. There are many cable phone providers. The reason I use a phone provided by Cox directly is stability of the voice signal. I could just plug my phone into the router. But then I would be competing for bandwidth with five other neighbors. By using a dedicated VoIP phone, even though it's internet-based, my phone signal is prioritized before all my neighbors are able to use bandwidth. Theoretically your virtual video and audio calls minimally could be achieved with only 1 Mbps upload speed and about 3 Mbps download speed. But your goal should be to shoot for 3 Mbps upload and 10 Mbps download.

There are a few sites to test download speeds. One is Google Speed Test. Another is Ookla speed test. A third choice is Fast.com. Any of these will test your internet speed.

A 5G cell phone will become necessary in the future. 4G phones have been with us for years. 4G LTE was the fastest signal you could get before 2021. But now 5G has spread across America and makes 4G LTE snail-paced by comparison. While there are cell phone manufacturers advertising 5G, the fast 5G cell towers are limited. If you are lucky enough to have 5G reception, this will become a wonderful backup in case your home cable internet is down.

Recently I watched a news show hosted by a political commentator. He interviewed poll workers during Detroit's controversial presidential race. One woman, speaking from inside her car, actually had a better-quality signal than two other guests interviewed from their homes. As with many cell phones, the top right-hand corner of her screen showed a 5G connection. It was impressive. This should be your backup plan in case the worst happens.

A hotspot is your friend. Most cell phone services have a hotspot. You can connect the internet to your cell providing a very high speed. If your phone has a 5G connection, the hotspot can be as fast as 300 Mbps download and at least 30 Mbps upload.

The only negative is whether your hotspot has data limited. Depending on your plan, you probably have only 500 MB to 1 GB availability per month. After that, your hotspot could be terminated or the speed throttled down. So, the idea here is to only use it in a pinch. Make it your backup plan.

Audio and camera connections. I once read there are no mistakes, only lessons. In that case, I have learned a lot of lessons, such as not using a new microphone on an important call without testing it first. Or using a camera that worked when I set it up, but neglected to test using a virtual platform.

Pay attention to these rules when setting up new audio and video connections.

If you can't see your device in the platform settings, it prob-ably won't work. I use a Sennheiser mic and earbuds. I decided the headphones may be too distracting and plugged in the Bose noise-canceling earbuds I use on airplanes. I use this method so often that I assumed it would work on my virtual platform as well. It didn't. I embarrassingly had to fumble with it during a client call. And then call the client back using my cell. He was understanding, but when you are limited on time, this kind of mistake can be a sales killer.

Test your devices on the virtual platform before your call. It's actually a helpful idea to record your call and listen to it after making any audio or video changes. You not only listen to the quality, but also check out framing and background. Even though you are only testing a new mic or camera, you will be surprised how many other distractions you will notice. There may be laundry on the couch behind you. There may even be a lighting hot spot in the wrong place. There is a reason why studio crews take hours before a shoot to get everything right.

Turn off all competing internet devices. Even if your home has fast internet, you never know when there could be band-width competition. All your neighbors might be streaming video at the same time as your call. Your provider might have speed issues. All of this redounds to the notion that you must reserve enough bandwidth to make your call effective. Turn off streaming music, video, or any other bandwidth-hogging sources at your location.

I play music in my office but am keenly aware of bandwidth. I use a SiriusXM receiver located in my bookcase. It gets a satellite signal in a visual line of sight through a window. The receiver is connected to speakers in my bookcase. I learned this bandwidth lesson in Portugal. Since internet is so variable outside the US, I noticed that virtual call quality would become inconsistent when any other device was on. Playing background internet-sourced music through a Bluetooth speaker would hog enough bandwidth to cause even audio call issues.

That also means turning off any device that could soak up bandwidth. You don't want to take the risk of a call turning bad because of technical issues.

Put a Do Not Disturb sign on the door. At a hotel this becomes obvious. I often forget that housekeeping will try to walk in to clean my room at any time. Even before the internet and virtual calls, you needed a DND sign if you wanted to sleep past 7:30 a.m. But today you don't want to disrupt the call only to tell a housekeeper knocking at the door to come back later.

Today, I put a DND even on my home office door. Everyone in my home is aware that when the door is closed, I am probably on a virtual call. But I don't even want anyone to knock on my door to find out.

Put your cell on silent. It's unprofessional when even broadcast show guests interrupt their appearances with a loud cell ring. I am sure that every broadcast producer has a list of dos and don'ts for guests. Like comb your hair and look in the mirror. But if a cell rings or dings, all participants should know better.

I have spent too many hours reshooting video because I forgot to disconnect my phone landline. I might be thirty minutes into a shoot, but all taping is wasted when the phone rings or beeps. On a hot day I would open the French doors to my usually quiet neighborhood, only to again waste time reshooting when a loud truck goes by.

Check the mirror before every call. You would always do this before appearing on a broadcast TV show. But do you take the same care checking yourself out before a virtual call? Is your collar up? Is your shirt inside out? Something on your face or a piece of hair out of place?

After a major speech years ago, I spent an hour signing books at the end of a presentation. A woman said she liked the speech but felt distracted. One of my pocket flaps was tucked inside awkwardly. She was so distracted that she had trouble listening. You don't want to take the chance that a caller will be distracted.

During one news show recently, the physician guest tried to show how to wear an N95 mask. But it was hooked to his microphone. He spent precious broadcast time in front of two million viewers trying to untangle himself.

Close all your browser tabs. While we all have Outlook, Chrome, and Excel spreadsheets open during calls, you don't want callers spying on your work.

During one webinar I attended, the host did a SlideShare on Zoom. The problem was that he selected from many open tabs. One showed his Word document negotiating a job with a competitor. Everyone on the call could see it. I can only imagine the conversation between him and the boss about his future employment plans.

It's also prudent to practice sharing slides before the call. Even if you know the virtual platform, you want to make the call seamless. Searching for a command or tab only creates distraction.

An important item to consider is how to end the virtual call. Sometimes, call participants simply say they need to go. Others just end the call. In most cases, the end of the call is a verbal goodbye followed by fumbling to find the end button on the virtual platform.

The most elegant way to end a call is to summarize and recap the main points. For example, you might say, "Thanks everyone for your time today. We covered three main points: how to send the seminar invitations, when to follow up with a call, and how to ask them to invite guests. I will send a follow-up email. Let's meet next Wednesday at two to finish this. Talk to you then," (and then push the end call button on your virtual platform).

The 5Ps: Prior Planning Prevents Poor Performance

My college tennis coach always said, "Kerry, remember the 5Ps." Whether it was remembering to serve and volley, step in on returns, move sideways when hitting overheads, or even remembering to bend my knees on a half volley, the 5Ps was a metaphor for everything.

The 5Ps in the virtual sale world means to check your internet connection and speed first thing in the morning. If there is a downed cable signal, it will probably happen overnight. Make sure your camera is operating effectively. Check to see that you have enough storage space in your computer or cell phone. With the cloud, it is easy to offload any storage needs to free up space on your laptop or cell.

When I'm in a hotel room trying to make coaching calls, I always test the internet connection both the night before and the morning of. Most new hotels have 10 Mbps download and about 1 Mbps upload speed. But for every hotel with strong internet, there are twenty others with slow or no internet at all. In addition, there are often thirty rooms on your floor sharing the same bandwidth. So, I want to test out the speed both the evening when I arrive and again when I wake up in the morning. I want to see how variable the speed is.

Wi-Fi Issues

Many virtual participants use Wi-Fi. It's convenient. The router may be 1,000 feet away. They may want to call from a backyard or even a back bedroom while the kids are playing. But Wi-Fi is too important to leave to chance. You need to hard wire the internet connection to your laptop. It is the only way you can ensure consistent speed and clarity.

One of my clients uses his laptop for our virtual calls. Some days the connection is crystal clear. Other days his face is pixelated and audio garbled. It is all because of Wi-Fi. Always connect an ethernet cord to and from your router to the laptop for every call. Today, most homes are wired only to the modem, not the router. Wireless is popular. You may have to extend a long line from the router to your laptop. Unless every room is hard wired, this old-fashioned set-up may still be the best one to ensure clear and fast signals.

The same is true of hotel rooms. Most of them now have Wi-Fi. Some are discontinuing ethernet hook-ups since so few guests use them. Don't make important calls from Wi-Fi. If you wouldn't chance Wi-Fi in your home, why would you take the risk of an important call being dropped or diminished in a hotel room. If your room doesn't have a cord, ask for one from the front desk. Better yet, carry a fast Cat8 cord in your bags. The virtual call is about connecting physically and emotionally, not about just making the call.

No matter how fast your cell connection, it's not as robust as cable internet. If someone is paying me hundreds of dollars per call for coaching, the least I can do is use a robust connection. It is super embarrassing to experience dropped coaching calls. Even if I'm in a parking lot, the sound quality on my cell will never be as good as a landline. If I'm calling staff to check up on a project, it doesn't matter. But when making a virtual sales call to a prospect or client, the distraction is not worth the risk.

Many years ago, I referred business to five other coaches. They all were proficient in knowing our systems. They were all excellent communicators. But one, Tim, preferred to use his cell to make coaching calls on the way to and from the office. After a few complaints, I told him that either he calls from a landline or I would refer future clients to the other coaches. Tim never quite got the message and didn't receive any more business from me.

Treat every virtual sales call as valuable and as important as you can make it. You don't need your cell phone to be scratchy. You don't need calls to be dropped. You don't want the prospect to ask you to repeat yourself multiple times during the call. The virtual call is about being professional. Even if the prospect or client uses a cell, you need to use a landline if you want to have a chance at making a sale. You don't need friction from a bad audio or video connection. Let the prospect apologize for being unprepared. Don't you be.

4

Virtual Presentations

There is a big difference between the structure of a video call and a virtual presentation. A virtual sales call needs to be interactive. You should never talk for more than ninety seconds without using a tie-down. You will recall, these are mechanisms you can use to keep the listener engaged. Examples of tie-downs are "Won't it?" "Doesn't it?" "Do you agree?" and "Does that make sense?" These are not invitations to start the prospect on a monologue. It is only a way to make sure that you don't talk too much.

A virtual video or audio presentation is one that keeps the listener engaged throughout the meeting. There is a difference in speaking to one or a hundred attendees. You may be doing a product presentation, demo, or even just presenting your service benefits.

I will offer a lot more advice later about how to speak at virtual events. When you are speaking to more than three people, you have to engage the group every ten minutes with rhetorical questions, call on names randomly, use humor, and even tell stories. When communicating with one to three listeners, you can ask for interaction and let them go. Remember, the listener always controls the conversation by the questions they ask. You can direct the agenda and timing simply by asking the right questions and being prepared to keep the answers direct and relevant.

Above all, keep every prospect engaged. Don't pitch. Always stay relevant in presenting ideas and concepts that are solutions to their needs. Don't make the mistake of thinking everyone wants to hear about your product or service. What they want to hear about are solutions. Here are a couple of ideas that will make your presentations a lot more focused, elegant, and successful.

Show Your Face

It's really tempting to do a presentation using SlideShare only. Your first thought might be to put PowerPoint on the screen and just speak on the bullet points. That is a big mistake. The presentation is not about the slides. It is about you and your prospect or client. It is about your ability to generate rapport and trust. Product solutions are always second. SlideShare and PowerPoint are only ways to illustrate you and your message. It is not the whole show.

If you are using SlideShare on any platform including Zoom, Webex, or even Google Meet, always make sure that your face is on the screen. I listened to a YouTube lecture recently on a medical issue. The lecture started with the title slide and moved through twenty more throughout the thirty-minute presentation. I never saw the speaker's face once. I suppose it was better than just reading a book. But any level of rapport was lost. If the prospect only cared about product solutions and price, you would be out of a job. It is your ability to generate rapport, listen for needs, and match those needs to solutions that makes you sought after and highly paid.

Sales is the highest-paid hard work and the lowest-paid easy work in the world. The easy part is product knowledge. The hard part is effectively using people skills. People skills are a lot more than social graces. They are the highest-level sales skills you can use. Think of it. You have the ability to communicate so well that people are willing to pay you an enormous amount of money. They buy from you even when they could get a discount from someone else. It's all about your ability to communicate that makes you valuable. Salespeople have always earned the highest income among any careers in the world—even more than physicians and lawyers. Most venture capitalists and Fortune 500 CEOs say their sales skills are the most valuable.

Sales and people skills depend on your ability to connect with people. Never hide your face.

The sale is never about the product or pricing. It is always about you. My friend Anthony Parinello, author of the book *Selling to VITO the Very Important Top Officer*, told a story about working for a major computer company at the beginning of his career. My alma mater, UCSD, called a few vendors to bid on a mainframe computer system. Tony worked for Honeywell at the time and knew his product was not the cheapest, but they did have the best solutions. When the UCSD provost handed out the Request for Proposal

(RFP), Tony knew he was not price competitive. He handed the RFP to the provost and said, "Are you selecting for price or cost?"

The provost asked what the difference was. Tony said, "Price is what you pay right now. Cost is what you pay over the long term." The provost handed a new RFP to the competitors and said he changed the selection criteria. He was now looking for price and cost. Needless to say, Tony and his company got the contract. That was not done from pitching the prospect or lowering the price. It took not only a relationship, but Tony's ability to listen for needs and present solutions that earned the sale.

Even though a new technology is used today, the relationship and solution are still everything. Your people skills will never be replaced. The technology may change, but the reasons people buy will always stay the same.

The 333 Presentation Process

In any presentation, virtual or not, you need to stay organized. Most of the presentations I have listened to have been absolutely terrible. Much of the time, the salesperson merely wants to communicate his product knowledge. Sometimes, a salesperson is willing to listen for openings in order to communicate his product knowledge. But it is the rare sales pro, virtual or not, who tailors product or service knowledge to solve relevant problems.

One of the best ways to present solutions on a virtual call is to use the 333 presentation process. Most of the new salespeople I work with tend to wing it. It's important to stay structured and organized in any presentation you run. During the probing stage of the sale, you can listen for needs and afford to take time to go down a few rabbit holes as you find out what the prospect really wants and needs.

The presentation stage is different. Especially in the virtual sale, you have to stay organized, succinct, brief, and relevant if you want your closing ratio to be above 20 percent. Most of my clients close about 90 percent of the prospects they choose to do business with. I believe about 10 percent of the population have the "right to remain stupid." They don't have the ability to make cogent and logical decisions. But for the rest of us, presenting in an organized, systematic way will dramatically increase your closing ratio. The 333 presentation process will do that for you. Here it is:

1. State the need.
2. Present a solution to that specific need.
3. Tell a story illustrating your solution.

Then trial-close.

I stated earlier that one single need generates a 36 percent chance of a sale. Two needs equal a 56 percent chance, and three needs gives you a 93 percent chance of producing business. Four needs become overkill and creates diminishing returns. Four needs will produce less than a 30 percent closing ratio. The reason is confusion. When the prospect gets confused, they want more information to gain understanding. When they get too much information, they become paralyzed and do nothing. It's up to you to package the solution and match your ideas to their needs in a simple, succinct, and organized way.

Let's talk about the structure of the virtual closing presentation. The first step is to develop rapport. Chat about the weather or even what the prospect did over the weekend. The next step is to then recap the three needs you discovered from the probing appointment.

After you recap, it's important then to trial-close. I discussed this process earlier. A trial close is a way to gain commitment to a solution. If you talk about a need and present the solution, it's important that the prospect immediately says yes or no to it. Most producers talk for thirty minutes and then ask if the prospect likes it. They are on pins and needles during the whole presentation time hoping the prospect will say yes. That is wrongheaded thinking.

You need to get commitment after every solution. You also need to break up the solutions, only addressing one need at a time. Then trial-close after each solution. This way you will gain agreement throughout the presentation, instead of waiting until the end to determine if you were successful.

The Up Front Close

Before you start the 333 closing presentation process, it's important to use the up front close. Have you ever been stalled? Has anybody ever said, "Let me think about it?" Here is a basic truth. If you ever let a prospect stall, they will. It is worse than wasting your time. If a prospect ever asks to take some time to think about your solution, you will be compelled to be polite and acquiesce. Unfortunately, they will forget 70 percent of your solution after one day and 90 percent after three days. They will be unable to make a decision of any kind after three days. They just can't remember the cogent and important information and details of the solution.

Here is what you will do as a follow-up. You will first leave a voicemail asking them to call you back. The next day you will leave another voicemail, followed by three more voicemails over the next week. Finally, you will catch the prospect on the phone and ask if they have made a decision. They will say, "Oh, I meant to call you last week. We decided to go a different direction." This doesn't mean they found a better solution. It only means they decided to buy the product or service that is best remembered. It will usually be the solution they heard most recently.

I will prove it to you. Can you remember a prospect who decided to buy a solution inferior to yours? You reminded them of your superior solution benefits and they said, "Oh, I forgot about that." But since they committed to buy from your competitor, they won't reconsider. Either way, the stall is death.

Isn't bad breath better than no breath at all? Isn't a prospect who says no immensely better than one that makes you chase them for two weeks, eventually still saying no? Think of this as taking crisp $100 bills out of your pocket and throwing them in the trash. It's not about spending the time following up. It's about how much time you are wasting when you could be prospecting for new business.

At first, you may be terrified with the risk of pushing the prospect to say no. You don't want to be rude. But there are ways of asking for honesty and candor that every prospect will respect.

Here is an example of the up front close:

Before we talk about some of these solutions, I just want to let you know that if you like this approach, I hope you say yes, let's do it. If for any reason it doesn't make sense, I want you to say no. You are not going to hurt my feelings. But what I would rather you not do is to say, let me take a few weeks, or tell me that you will get back to me next month. Because that only tells me you don't have enough information to make an informed decision. And again, I would rather you just say no. Is that okay with you?

There are many nuances important to use with the up front close.

Be direct. If you seem embarrassed, your prospect may also feel awkward in giving you an answer. Be direct and polite. Asking them to make a decision will not automatically push them into saying no. But it will give them the permission to be candid.

Make sure they give you an answer. It will be tempting for you to say the up front close, but not wait for an answer. Pause long enough for them to agree. I have made this mistake many times only to get a stall later, having failed to initially get a verbal commitment.

Don't sell to someone who won't buy. Often, if the virtual prospect won't agree to tell you yes or no, they are just shopping. Regardless, ask why they can't make a decision. Sometimes, they have already decided to buy from somebody else. Other times they are just doing research waiting to buy much later. Regardless, you should never waste your time selling to somebody who can't or won't make a decision to buy. You also can't awkwardly stop the meeting when you find out they won't make a decision. What should you do?

The answer is to give a 30,000-foot overview on how you might be different from your competitors and perhaps address some generalities of what solution you would recommend when you next meet. For example, "Retirement planning is really about protecting you from volatility, decreasing taxes, minimizing inflation, making your money last as long as you do, and leaving a legacy for your family. When we get back together in a few months, I want to drill down on exactly how we can put these five factors into your retirement plan. When is a good time to follow up for you?"

Most of the time, your prospect will give you a follow-up time. Once in a while they will lay a trap. They will push you for a price. You need to resist the temptation by saying, "I don't really know that right now. When we get back together, I will put together a plan that outlines all the costs. Is that okay with you?"

If necessary, give them a range. I will never quote a price to a meeting planner unless they are willing to make a decision. But sometimes when there is a committee, I ask to talk to the committee head. As a last resort, I will say that my speaking fees are between $7,500 and $12,000. When they are ready, I can narrow my fee to what their budget is and what they actually want. Rarely do I get pushback.

Don't sell to people who can't buy. They will often take your solutions and pricing to another competitor. There is no up side in presenting to somebody who can't commit to a decision. I know you will feel tempted to present a solution that will knock their socks off. You will be so impressive that even if they tell you up front they want to stall, your amazing brilliance will change their mind. You are simply deluding yourself and wasting time.

Many years ago, I gave a speech to a mortgage group in New York City. An attendee filled out our coaching evaluation sheet and asked to talk to me. The next Friday we spoke for twenty minutes. I found three needs he wanted solutions to. Before I presented coaching, I did the up front close. He said he couldn't make a decision and would have to talk to his wife. Normally, if I had known he would stall, I would not have presented more than a basic overview of what coaching is. I certainly would not have given him a price.

But I had been doing the up front close for so many years that I decided to change things up. I did the presentation, gave him a price, and we agreed to talk at 9:00 a.m. the next Monday morning. I sent a follow-up email as a reminder. I received a response from the prospect less than five minutes later telling me he did not want to do coaching. It is good that he responded so quickly. But this was simply another confirmation that a stall now just means a no later. They have taken hundreds of dollars out of your pocket by making you chase them. Use the up front close. Risk the prospect saying no. Encourage them to be candid and honest. It's a lot better than wasting your time and money.

Part of the 333 strategy is to use a story to illustrate your solution. Facts tell, stories sell. People never buy features, benefits, or even pricing. They always buy rapport and trust. Usually trust comes from emotion. The only technique I have ever seen that communicates emotion in a short period of time is telling a story. Think of all the skilled motivational speakers who have made an impact on you. Was it a turn of phrase? Was it their enthusiasm? Or was it a story you connected with? Stories are everything. If you really want to capture somebody emotionally, tell a story. The most successful sales pros I have ever worked with are master storytellers.

Colors

One aspect of virtual video presentations completely ignored is colors. Do you think color has any impact on a prospect or client's perception? Do graphics you use during a virtual video presentation have any impact on the prospect's emotions? Do you think the colors you wear influence your client's decisions in any way?

Every time I do a speech on how color impacts buyer behavior, I always ask audiences which Porsches go faster? Brown or red ones? After the audience laughs, I then ask which pickup trucks are more rugged and sturdy? Red or brown ones? Now the audience gets it. Every car owner knows that red goes faster. Have you ever heard the phrase, "Arrest me red?" Don't red cars just look faster?

On a Porsche dealer's lot in Long Beach, California, in 2015, Merita and I were in the market for a new Cayenne S. There were many to choose from. But one in particular had all the extras I wanted. Heated steering wheel, heated seats, side and rear radar, and even an amazing Bose sound system. The only problem was the color. It was red. My wife loved it. All I could say to her was, "Do you have any idea how many tickets we are going to get in this car?"

She laughed and said, "Why don't you just drive the speed limit?" One of my tennis buddies sarcastically said that cops will never notice me speeding in a red Porsche. The red Porsche Cayenne S looked like it was speeding ten miles over the limit, standing still.

Here's another question. Stop signs are red, correct? What is the background color of yield signs? Yellow? But the answer is still red. Most statutes changed yield signs to red in the 1970s because so few motorists would even notice a sign in yellow.

The California prison system for many years employed a unique way of dealing with aggressive, unruly inmates. They employed pink cells. Pink is a very calming color. When a prisoner goes crazy, whacked out, nuts, they put him in a pink cell for thirty minutes. Generally, after this time-out, the prisoner walks out much calmer than when he walked in.

Hayden Fry, the legendary coach of the Iowa Hawkeyes football team, had a perfect winning streak at home in the 1980s. Among his many secrets then, and today, are the locker rooms. The home locker room is painted in blue. Guess what the visitor locker room color is? You got it. Pink!

While most of us recognize color has an impact in clothing, home design, and packaging, few of us understand what kind of impact it has on buyer behavior. Color affects you in two ways.

1. What you associate color with. What does the color remind you of? If you see someone wearing a black suit, do you think of a waiter? A funeral? A maître d'? If you see someone in green camouflage, do you think of the military? The symbols we think in and associate emotions with also have colors. The color and shape of a stop sign is a good example. When we see red, it is nearly always associated with caution and danger. These colors impact us both positively and negatively.

2. How color affects you physiologically. Have you ever heard the phrase, "I was so angry, I could see red?" Color also affects you physiologically. In one research project done in the 1980s, mobiles were dangled over baby cribs in both pink and red. As you might've guessed, the babies looking up at red were much more active than the babies seeing pink.

There is a substance made by the pituitary gland called melanin. There is a large amount contained in the iris of the eye. People with brown eyes have the greatest amount of melanin. Coincidentally the color that has the greatest irritating impact on melanin is yellow. Slides, notepads, or even backgrounds in yellow will create iris discomfort in those people with the greatest concentrations of melanin. Yet, in most cases, salespeople like you are likely to outline their ideas on either a white or yellow pad. Not knowing that the yellow color may be irritating and possibly headache-provoking may be a problem for those prospects who are sensitive.

THE THREE BEST COLORS
Three colors are more persuasive to your prospects than any others in the spectrum. These colors affect your prospects and clients both physiologically and emotionally. I recommend you wear

these colors, put your virtual video slides in these colors, and even decorate your website in these colors. Here are the three most persuasive colors you can use in a business environment.

Navy Blue

This is the most popular color in the spectrum. It is also the favorite color of both males and females in America. Many decades ago, the biggest computer company in the world, IBM, decided on a nickname that would impact their brand. Not only did IBM'ers want a memorable phrase, it required a color that everybody would recognize. IBM spent millions creating the name Big Blue.

Did you notice I use the shade navy instead of just blue? This is because of its impact on high-net-worth affluent buyers. The more money people make, the more muted their color preferences. If you visit extremely high-net-worth communities like Atherton, California; Darien, Connecticut; or even the Cherry Hills community near Denver, Colorado, homes are usually painted in a muted tone. You will only see pastels and bright colors in less affluent neighborhoods.

Dove Gray

This color is also associated with affluence. *Inc.* magazine annually publishes their list of the 500 wealthiest people in the world. The cover issue is always dove gray. This also happens to be a formal color. Dove gray suits are conservative. Even a dove gray tie with a tuxedo looks good. Dove gray is the color of conservatism, social economic status, and affluence.

In 2006, I bought a new Porsche 911s Cabriolet convertible. I had been waiting eighteen months for it to be delivered from Germany. I became impatient and saw one in the local newspaper (back in the old days). It had navy blue paint on the body and a dove gray top. I thought it was gorgeous. In negotiating with the salesperson, I discovered it had been on the lot for three months with no offers. The salesperson said Porsche owners are fickle. They want one of only three colors: black, white, or silver (dove gray). But for some reason a dove gray top was not acceptable. To me, it was the best of all worlds. It encompassed the two colors most persuasive to the affluent. I still own it and, after fifteen years, receive many compliments.

Hunter Green

This color was popular twenty years ago as well as today. It is a perpetually popular color. Think of the locations you are most likely to see hunter green. They are country clubs, affluent restaurants, and high-net-worth nightclubs. What do you associate hunter green with? Money, affluence, and wealth. Hunter green ties aren't known to be popular. In his book *Dress for Success*, John T. Molloy explicitly recommended not to wear green suits. While I accept his expert opinion, hunter green is an amazing color to use in your virtual presentations, websites, and even business cards.

My oldest daughter bought me a green hat from the most famous golf tournament in America, The Masters. My wife said she never saw me wear a green golf hat before. If you are a golfer, any hat color besides green displaying The Masters wouldn't be appropriate. The affluent symbol of the tournament in Augusta, Georgia, is green. In fact, the tournament winner even gets a green jacket. Most golfers seeing a green blazer, even in San Diego, would be reminded of The Masters.

THE THREE WORST COLORS

Here are the colors you should avoid. Don't let people focus on these colors, or notice even a passing image. Don't forget, colors affect you physiologically and associatively. This means when people see one of these colors, they may be impacted negatively and unconsciously. Avoid these colors in your slides, virtual room background, websites, and even brochures.

Black

This negative color is easy to understand. We associate black with death and dying around the world. In fact, burials are almost always decorated in black. The only funeral color in the world other than black is white. And that color is only prevalent at Chinese funerals. Black can also cause depression within minutes of looking at it.

An interesting side note is that of Yakuza crime family funerals. Attendees are dressed in black. But the head of the family wears white. This denotes a type of purity from the head of the family.

There is a subtle way to use black. And that is when a color is superimposed, or reversed out of it. For example, if there is an image with a black background, the color may not be noticed. But if black is used to accentuate or illustrate, your prospect or client may feel a negative impression.

Purple

This is the color I get the most pushback on. My female speech attendees always tell me they love purple. Male audiences often tell me purple shirts are among their favorites. But the research shows that purple is not the right color in business. Think about why.

A service member in the military gets a Purple Heart when they are wounded in action. A purple cloth is draped over the cross in a Christian church as a symbol of mourning during Easter. Purple is my granddaughter Cora's favorite color. In spite of my attitude that anything Cora likes I like, purple is a bad color to use in a business environment. What people associate purple with is negative. You do not want to take the chance of that kind of impact on a prospect or client.

Yellow

This could be the worst of the worst. Yellow causes anxiety faster than black produces depression. When placed in yellow rooms, detainees become irritated. Just as the melanin pigment of the eye is irritated by yellow, the color will impact your prospects physiologically. It also has a negative connotation. Decades ago, when someone was labeled a coward, they were called yellow.

As you can see, the best colors to use in your business are the ones that impact affluent people the most. This doesn't mean the less affluent don't notice these colors or are not emotionally impacted by them. It just means that if you are going to use colors to enhance persuasiveness, make sure they are appealing to your most discerning prospects.

This also means when you're tempted to use color, don't depend on prospects or clients telling you what they like. Because colors impact people unconsciously, they might experience emotions they can't explain. If I'm at a funeral, I might feel sad. Is it because of the colors at the funeral? Or is it the event in general? Does the loss of a friend cause sadness and black enhances the emotion? Also, does seeing a black suit bring me back to the emotions of being at a funeral?

Use the three most persuasive colors during your virtual presentations. Avoid the least effective colors. This will allow you to focus on the aspects of the virtual presentation you can control like framing, sound, content, and other areas that will increase your communication success.

Be Relevant

One temptation most virtual salespeople fall prey to is talking too much about themselves and their company. It's obvious in the beginning of a relationship that you need to establish credibility and confidence. But when you talk too much about yourself throughout the presentation, any extra discussion about your competency becomes irrelevant and redundant.

I have discussed earlier why you need a short elevator speech. An elevator speech is a one- to two-minute message explaining who you are and what you do, followed by a story illustrating your expertise. After the story, you need a segue addressing its relevance to your prospect. The only time you should ever discuss yourself after the elevator speech is when the prospect asks a direct question. Everything else should be related to how your solution will satisfy their needs.

Often when I role-play virtual presentations with coaching clients, I hear them effectively address solutions to needs in the beginning of the presentation. But soon they go back to, "My company is better than anybody in the industry at—" or "We have more experience in dealing with this kind of concept than all our competitors." At some point the prospect will feel pitched.

Your goal in doing a virtual presentation is to explain how and why the solution is a good fit. Not to discuss your personal brilliance. Don't let your company propaganda influence your presentation. They want you to feel confident in the products or services they make. But don't let that influence your message to the prospect unless it is relevant. Prospects need to know you are able to achieve their goals because of the expertise provided—not because you told them how wonderful you are.

Be Brief

During a face-to-face meeting, you can usually read body language if you are paying attention. If you have some level of emotional intelligence, you will be able to read facial emotions, interest, and even discern defensiveness.

For some reason during a virtual call, we tend to focus more on what to say than how people are receiving the message. On a virtual video or audio call, you can lose attention in a heartbeat. Attention spans are dramatically shorter on virtual calls than in face-to-face meetings because of too many distractions. Your prospect or client has a cell phone beckoning their attention. Their iPad is only inches away. I'm sure other devices are creating distraction. You have to be on top of your game if you want to keep their focus. You need to be brief.

Because of this, it's important to use tie-downs and engage the participant at least every three minutes. I discussed tie-downs earlier. These are ways to keep the listener attentive. For example, you could say, "Do you agree?" "Does this make sense?" or even, "What is your take on this idea?"

Don't forget, the listener always controls the conversation. The better you listen, the more you can direct the length and content of the virtual meeting. Sometimes virtual meetings go down rabbit holes of irrelevance. It's up to you to maintain control and stay on point. That is why you need to always focus and limit yourself to addressing solutions to only three needs.

Nobody will remember more than three points during a virtual presentation. Bringing your prospect back to three main points is always a great idea (the 333 Presentation Process already introduced). Those three points should reflect the needs you discover from the Five-Step Bridge (a technique I discuss soon). For example, if the need was to decrease market volatility in a retirement plan, the prospect may go down a rabbit hole and talk about their last vacation with the grandkids. While it's good to listen, it's also important for you to maintain control of the conversation. In other words, you might segue the discussion, "I'm sure your grandkids also want you to have a stable stream of income during retirement you can't outlive." This will allow them to spend more time with the grandkids and not have to be dependent on their own kids.

This is just one example of how the listener can always keep control. It is never the person who does all the talking that directs the agenda. It's the listener. You need to be that listener.

Great Listeners Have Three Traits
1. LISTENERS ARE CURIOUS.
When a client or prospect makes a comment about something unique in their life, great listeners are interested in finding out more. Great listeners want to make people feel understood. But they are also interested in learning new things. The skilled listeners believe every interaction has a gem to be mined. They just have to listen intently enough. There is something to be learned and benefited from. Poor listeners need to be hit over the head to value a conversation.

2. GREAT LISTENERS VALUE OTHERS' VIEWPOINTS AND EXPERIENCES.
One of my secrets in using social media is to invite anybody who wants to connect to speak on the phone for ten minutes. The responses I get are amazing. I will discuss this a lot more later in the chapter on social media. But, generally, I first ask how much they know about me. Few know more than my name. These, by the way, are people who ask to connect with me.

After an elevator speech, I always segue the conversation to find out more about them. At least 95 percent of these participants spend the call talking about themselves. It could be how smart they are, how marvelous their company is, or even to brag about their products. But rarely does anybody ask questions. They just don't seem to be curious. They are mesmerized with themselves. When you are as interested in your prospect or client as yourself, your production will go up. The more rapport you have, the more trust you will create. Rapport and trust are the reasons people buy. But it all starts with you being a great listener.

3. GREAT LISTENERS ALWAYS RECAP WHAT THEY HEAR.

Most salespeople think they have to be glib and persuasive. But a top sales producer will listen to a prospect or client and recap what they hear like a psychotherapist. If you've ever been to a marriage counselor or therapist, you have noticed them listen intently. They always make you feel understood. Their recap phrasing is always, "So if I understand correctly, you are frustrated with your job, wish your kids were better behaved, and would love it if your spouse didn't complain quite so much. Did I get all that right?" They will recap emotions before they suggest any solutions to concerns.

In a way, you are simply a highly paid psychotherapist. You are paid to listen intently for needs and show emotional intelligence by reading them nonverbally. You are paid to show empathy and understanding. Finally, you are paid to recap what you've heard. Only after people feel understood will they listen to your solutions. You are paid to use all these skills to increase your closing ratio.

According to U.S. Trust, a wealth management company, 86 percent buy because they feel understood, but only 6 percent buy because they are made to understand. Your closing ratio will increase dramatically if you first make sure that prospects are understood instead of making them understand. The way to do this is to listen.

How to Be Charismatic

Why are people so drawn to others? Why are *you* so drawn to some people and not others? Is it their enthusiasm? Is it that you feel welcomed and accepted? It's probably a mixture of all these. But most importantly, charisma is most quickly generated by capturing attention during all aspects of communication. Charismatic people have mixed voice inflection and vocal variety. They can paint pictures using stories to illustrate any concept. Charismatic people help you visualize any concept at any time. But above all, charismatic people are experts at engaging others.

Karl Rove, the political strategist and deputy chief of staff for former president George W. Bush, has this kind of charisma. Not only is he self-deprecating, his understanding and level of detail in communicating politics is more robust than any other Republican strategist. Rove laughs readily. He tells stories frequently. But his real gift is using graphics during all his interviews. This is one way he engages the audience. He is the only guest on cable who uses graphics. He is gifted at explaining sometimes difficult political calculations. He is also famous for using a whiteboard. Obviously, he knows what the agenda is before the show starts. But he usually outlines three concepts. He often fills in answers on the whiteboard as he responds.

Many TV hosts grouse sarcastically as Rove brandishes the whiteboard. Sean Hannity on Fox teases him, saying Rove needs a new whiteboard and that Hannity will buy one. While the teasing is good-natured, Rove always gets his points across. Good graphics combined with enthusiasm and knowledge focused toward making your listener feel understood is the definition of charisma.

You can try several ways to use graphics on your virtual platform calls. Of course, you can use the Karl Rove whiteboard. You can also use your hands to gesture. But it's easier using a virtual platform. Most allow you to use a virtual laser pointer when displaying slides. You simply can select the pointer with your mouse during the call. And even erase any circles or underlines when you are done talking. You really can show charisma any time you want.

How to Structure and Organize Virtual Presentations

One of the biggest roadblocks to successful virtual presentations is a lack of structure. Not even 1 percent of my new coaching clients have sufficient structure and effective systems in their business processes. When they ask for referrals, they use whatever words come to mind. They don't memorize the right way to ask. They just wing it. When they probe for needs, they ask general questions hoping they can connect well enough to learn what prospects want.

When they do virtual presentations, they go back to presenting the same benefits as they have for every other prospect. If they get lucky, the prospect will say yes. If they aren't lucky, the meeting will become one more statistic. Most don't have the right kind of systems to make yes a frequent response.

In my coaching practice, I always try to get clients to first learn to be systematic in best-practice processes. Everybody listens to me on a coaching call. After all, they are paying for it. But not many will practice those systems outside of our appointments. Those who do usually double their income. But most don't internalize the concepts and make them part of their business.

Status quo is the stickiest glue known to mankind. It's amazing the lengths people will go to keep doing what they've always done. It is probably because of their level of comfort. It's also likely their resistance to changing behavior. But those clients who learn and use systems frequently dramatically increase income without working more hours.

The system and structure of any virtual presentation needs to be consistent. As I discussed earlier, you need to construct the virtual sales closing presentation with these three steps:

1. Recap
2. Trial close
3. Up front close

The 333 Strategy

1. State the first need.
2. Present the solution to the first need.
3. Tell a story about another client who used that solution. Then trial-close to make sure the prospect agrees with the solution.

The process after that is to rinse and repeat. Go to need two and use the same structure. Then present a solution to need three using the same process. After you've given three solutions to three needs, do one final trial close.

Your closing ratio will approach 85 percent if you use this process. But you have to be systematic. You have to be structured. You can't wing anything on a virtual call. You can deviate and improvise when you want. But first you have to follow a system.

I am a spontaneous speaker. I love audience members who make comments while I am speaking. I also actually like hecklers. They give me a chance to engage the audience. I will listen and then good-naturedly tease the heckler. Even if they are malicious, I always have a comeback. The only time it becomes tedious is when they are drunk and malicious. But even then, it's fun to test my wit. If they become too obnoxious, other audience members will shut them down.

One particularly obnoxious speaker yelled out that my PhD means piled higher and deeper. He said psychology was the study of the id by the odd. Pretty funny. But I responded by asking the audience, "How many others here don't know what's going on yet today?" I smiled in response. The group erupted with laughter. The heckler even laughed.

All of this is only possible if I can quickly go from my improv back to the structured speech. I need to know where I left off almost like a bookmark left from the day before. This is the power of having a system when you do a virtual presentation. You need structure. You need to follow a system. Only then can you be more spontaneous and have fun. You can tease the audience or virtual call attendees. You always need a reference point to go back to. You have to have structure.

Dealing with Diversions

There are always roadblocks to every virtual presentation. Some are self-inflicted. Others will blindside you. One diversion you can avoid is to never send pricing materials before or during the meeting. If you send cost estimates in your handouts, callers will go to that page and be distracted for the rest of the meeting. Your product or service is either too expensive, or they will compare it to competitors', ignoring your presentation.

If you are using SlideShare, you can reveal pricing when you want. But if you send the presentation ahead of the call, the prospect will always click at the end of the file, looking for cost. Unless you are clearly the lowest price out there, the prospect will spend the rest of the meeting thinking about the price instead of the value you bring. Often, prospects will only hear the price and turn off everything else you say.

The other obstacle in any virtual call may be a diversion block. Perhaps a prospect interrupts, stating that your experience is insufficient. Perhaps they think you don't understand their system well enough. They may state a concern that you aren't local. But the biggest virtual presentation diversion will always be price. When this happens after your presentation, it is called an objection. But before or during the presentation, it's only a diversion.

Often in the middle of a presentation they may ask the price. The prospect can sound really convincing. They may say, "Before we go any further and waste any time, we want to know if we can afford it. How much does this cost?" If you answer before you have established value, you will lose. They will always say no or stall you. Without first establishing value, your price will always be too high.

The right way to deal with a diversion block is to deflect it to when you are ready. Address the diversion by saying, "That is a great question. But I need to find out more before I can present the right price." Or you can say, "I have no idea. There are several options. If I can learn more about you first, I can talk about what it will cost. Is that okay with you?"

PRICE SHOPPING

One of the most difficult diversions to overcome is when prospects ask about price without knowing your value. Often, they will ask how much you would hypothetically charge for a service or product. Sometimes you will get an email asking for pricing. Never, ever, ever fall for this. Unless you are selling a $15 bottle of wine, don't quote a price.

There are only a couple of reasons prospects ask about price before they hear about value:

- The prospect is price shopping. They are trying to find a range of prices because they have no idea how much a product or service will cost.
- They received another quote and wonder if it's competitive. They never planned on using your services. They only want to find out whether the price they were already quoted is fair.
- They aren't ready to buy. They are only shopping for a product or service in the distant future. This could be a waste of your time.

Regardless of the reason, don't ever quote a price without first probing for needs. Then present a solution. I know it seems tempting to quote price. You don't want to lose business. But the bottom line is you will rarely ever get a sale based only on price. There are exceptions. If I'm shopping for tires and know the exact brand and size, price makes a difference. It's all I need to make a buying decision. If I'm shopping for a Bluetooth pair of earbuds, and know that the Bose Quiet Comfort 20 is the model I want, all I care about is getting the lowest price for the fastest delivery.

But you are not selling a cheap commodity; otherwise you would not be reading this book. You are selling your services or a product using expertise. You need to find out the needs of the prospect and client and which solution will work best for them. You don't need to act like an electronics store sales associate.

Recently I had a paid membership to eSpeakers, a marketing website. It is free to be listed, but $500 a year to display biography, topics, demo videos, and testimonials based on a keyword search. I paid for the listing for three years with absolutely no leads. A week before I called to cancel, I received a request for a price quote. The company wanted to know my speaking fee for an October conference of 500 attendees. I sent an email asking for a short ten-minute phone conversation. The prospect refused and asked again for my price. I mentioned that I couldn't give him a speaking fee unless I could learn more about the conference. What would you have done in this situation? Would you risk losing the sale?

We sent emails back and forth a few more times. He was in a new position and had no idea how much speakers charged. He was only trying to put together a budget for the next meeting and wouldn't pick speakers for another six months. You might make the case that if he thought my speaking fee was in his budget, I could have engaged him later when ready. But since he didn't know his budget, or even the topic, it would've been a total waste of time.

Don't ever quote a price unless you can first establish value. The only way to establish value is to probe for needs and make sure that your solution is one that matches the need.

The Only Way to Say Less Is to Speak Longer

The most important aspect in delivering a virtual or any other presentation is to be brief. In fact, the virtual presentation is more abbreviated than a face-to-face version. Never think your prospect will listen as long as you want to talk. A few years ago, a financial advisor brought in two technical experts presenting an innovative retirement concept called a Welfare Thrift Plan. It had the feature of allowing contributions of more than $100,000 pre-tax, far beyond what would be allowed in a normal IRA.

I remember walking into the expert's office and chatting over a cup of coffee for a few minutes. For the next sixty minutes, I heard one expert talk about various plans, tax implications, legal and accounting fees, and anything else he decided to fit in the presentation. It was the most boring hour I've ever had to sit through. It was much like the line, "That's an hour out of my life I will never get back."

It is so tempting to think that a prospect will be rapt with attention as you present. But even the best speakers with the most charisma can really only command about ten minutes of attention. You need to engage using tie-downs and use participation.

Many years ago, one of my friends asked me to listen to a sales presentation for his client, Allergan pharmaceuticals. He was their meeting planner. The president and senior vice president were in the room listening along with me. My friend, Scott, introduced the vendor to us. At that point the salesperson went on for nearly an hour without ever engaging the executives. At the very end of the presentation, the president said, "Great presentation. We will get back to you." The vendor thanked him and that was the end of the meeting.

The president looked at me and asked what I thought. I deflected and asked instead what his impression was. I didn't know much about the product or the needs. He said, "A total waste of time. The vendor didn't address any of our concerns." The whole team then walked out of the office. I was struck by how easy it would've been for the vendor to recap needs, trial-close, reference those needs, and then do a polite up front close.

Sales can be tough. Booking an hour with the president of a major company is an opportunity we all want. To waste that chance by not having an effective systematic presentation is truly a nightmare. Please keep in mind your prospect or client has less than a ten-minute attention span. If you can remember that, your closing ratio will go up.

How to Do a Virtual Demo

During COVID-19, car dealers tried to do virtual tours of their models. Furniture salespeople attempted Zoom conferences showing couches, end tables, and even bedroom sets. Real estate agents did virtual tours guiding you through their listings. Financial advisors engaged clients in Zoom calls showing illustrations of retirement plans. It seems as though we were all doing things that are "almost like being there."

But virtual tours and demos are not just substitutes for being face-to-face. These meetings need to be interactive. The real estate agent who tours a house using Webex can't act as if it's just them and their cell phone. They need to use the same engagement as if physically taking a couple through the house.

For example, the agent might have a virtual conversation on the porch before entering the front door. They might start by discussing the buyer's three needs and ask what they want to see first. The agent then might open the lockbox on the front door and do a minimal tour of the living room and kitchen. But since the buyer cares most about a view, an office, and library, the tour would initially focus on those areas. Little time would be spent touring the part of the house the potential buyer cares least about. A savvy agent will focus on what the buyer needs and wants while recognizing how limited their attention span is.

A life insurance agent doing a virtual call could run a demo in much the same way. They would first discover three things the prospect wants most. These could be the death benefit, college funding by borrowing against cash value, and avoiding taxes by using life insurance in a retirement plan. There are a lot of benefits provided by life insurance products. But the savvy virtual presenter will address the buyer's needs first. If the buyer has any questions beyond those needs, the agent can then address any other areas of interest. But the savvy agent will never talk about a benefit the prospect didn't specifically ask for. Mistakes are not made by being too brief. Sales errors are made by talking too much about irrelevant information.

MICRO DEMOS THAT SELL

Many years ago, I started doing short three-minute demos advertising one of my future speeches. My home studio utilizes a camera, box lighting, and a green screen directly behind. The short demo usually includes a twenty- to thirty-second elevator speech followed by three bullet points that I will address during my conference speech.

In the end, I tell the listener the meeting location, date, and time. Surprisingly, the short three-minute demos have a huge impact on how many people attend. Without the video demo, attendees would show up based on the title of the speech in the conference agenda. With a demo, an audience member may be attracted to a lot more than just the topic. Attractions hopefully include my delivery, background, and bullet points—all of which promise what the audience will gain as a result of spending an hour during the presentation.

These brief demos are not just effective in attracting audiences to a speech. They are also effective in selling myself as a speaker. Before talking with the meeting planner, I always send my website URL, hoping they watch my ten-minute demo video on the first page. Few do. Later, I started recording short three-minute videos with the prospect's logo on the green screen in the background. I would do a quick elevator speech followed by a list of two or three presentations I think the prospect might be most interested in. I would segue to a story illustrating the kinds of points they may gain from the speech.

The end of the video is always that I look forward to talking to them referencing the date and time of our next virtual meeting. Nearly every prospect at least opens the three-minute video. Doing a virtual video introduction before an important prospect meeting will gain more attention, allocate more time to talk, and, of course, increase your closing ratio.

You're probably thinking that you don't have a green screen, don't own professional lighting, and certainly don't have a professional video camera. But mobile phone cameras today are just as good as professional production video was even two years ago. Your cell phone provides the same HD video quality short of broadcast TV or cinema. All you have to do is put your cell on a stand or selfie stick, make sure your Bluetooth earbuds are connected, and you have an instant studio.

Think of the advantage if you sent a short three-minute video to a new prospect with at least your elevator speech and what you typically do for your clients. Your business is about being unique. Your sales success is about differentiation. Without being different, the prospect will make you a commodity. If they can do that, they will find the cheapest version. You need to be different. You can be much more effective by engaging the prospect in a way that your competitors can't.

Death by PowerPoint

One secret the best presenters abide by is never putting too much information on a single slide. When too many words cloud the slide, it becomes death by PowerPoint. Amateur presenters will put everything possible on each slide. Bad presenters then often read the slide out loud eventually boring the audience.

Memorable presenters put information on a slide emblematic of a concept, and that's all. They will also never put more than two or three points on single slide. They will use only one or two words per bullet point.

A presentation is never about the words on a slide, it's always about you. Most presenters use keywords as memory joggers of what to say. They never read the slide. If the only message were the words on a slide, why would anyone want to listen to you? Why not just read a white paper or a document and avoid taking the time to view a virtual presentation?

I hate to overgeneralize, but medical speakers are some of the worst presenters to stand behind a lectern. They are untrained and believe the science is more important than the presentation. They have it half right. Both are important.

First, most medical speakers never leave the podium. The lectern distances and detaches the presenter from the audience. But worse yet, nearly everything they say is read from the slides. Sometimes the slides contain paragraphs. Other times, the charts and graphs are too small to read.

But poor speaking skills aren't limited to medical speakers. I was in Tucson at a financial conference. The creator of a new retirement software program spoke directly after my presentation. He had three paragraphs per slide that nobody, even in the first row, could read. He apologized multiple times for the small lettering. But not only were his slides unreadable, he stood behind a lectern. He failed to engage anybody in the audience. One by one, attendees left for bathroom and coffee breaks and never came back. He was down to only 25 percent of the audience in the first thirty minutes.

Here are a couple of tips in delivering any kind of virtual presentation or demo. Whether you are presenting to three or 300, these tips will make your message more persuasive.

1. INCLUDE AN AGENDA ON THE FIRST SLIDE.

Make it brief and concise. After you mention the agenda, ask if the attendees have anything they would like to add. Engage them immediately.

2. MAKE YOUR SLIDES RELEVANT TO THE AGENDA.

If a prospect wants to hear more than what you've advertised, be prepared to show slides in addition. I will usually add ten to twenty slides at the end of each virtual presentation. I have a printed list of the slides I can refer to. If someone has a question, I can just type the slide number in PowerPoint. The slide will pop up, and, viola, I can again address any item that is important to them.

3. PUT NO MORE THAN THREE BULLET POINTS ON EACH SLIDE.

Also put no more than three words per bullet point. The presentation is not the slides. It is you. Many years ago, I spoke to a group of 500 people. An AV technician at a major Las Vegas hotel insisted on darkening the room so the attendees could see the huge screen in the middle of the stage. I asked them to put the screen in the corner of the room and turn all the lights up. The AV expert was so irritated that he called over the meeting planner, my client, to intercede. He said the audience would not be able to see the screen. I looked directly at him and said assertively, "The presentation isn't the screen. It is me. The slides are only to illustrate what I talk about." When you have a hammer, you only focus on nails. He was an AV guy only concerned with sound and images.

I am often asked what makes a great speaker. The answer is your ability to connect with the audience. Poor speakers read their speeches behind a podium. Great speakers make eye contact and talk directly to individuals in the audience. The problem is your presentation may not be memorized and you need to refer to notes. This is not a problem as long as you ditch the podium. Your presentation should be in an outline format with key words or phrases for notes instead of sentences. This will force you to be more interactive instead of rote.

My youngest daughter, Catherine, was married in Denver on June 11, 2021. I watched these young millennials read speeches at both the rehearsal dinner and wedding reception. All of them read speeches and often talked about how nervous they were. I saw the DJ during dinner at the bar. I asked him how many weddings he had attended. He said 120 per year and mentioned he was booked two years in advance. I asked also how many fathers-of-the-bride speeches he had heard. He said thousands.

I asked how many he liked. He said three because they were short. I finally asked how many were presented by professional speakers. He said, "Only you." I asked how he knew I spoke for a living. He said, "Before the wedding, you checked all the microphones and walked around the room listening for dead spots. You looked for the best place to lay your notes so the group wouldn't notice you had any." He finally said, "You placed the notes at a table to be closer to the audience."

The way to use notes but also connect with the audience is to put them on the first table. If the event is theater style, get an attendee to place your notes on their lap so you can glance down when necessary. I recently watched a TED Talk and noticed the speaker glancing at notes on the floor. This is also a great idea to better connect. I have never done a TED Talk, but I don't think I would stay on the stage. I would jump down and walk in the crowd as I presented.

In a virtual setting, you have the ability to sit at your desk and present. But the concept remains that you still need to connect with the audience. If you use notes, make sure they are short memory joggers. If you read your presentation, it will be as boring as standing behind a podium reading your speech.

Some brilliant virtual speakers will present standing on a stage as if they were speaking to an in-person group. Every speaker gains energy by standing and presenting instead of sitting in front of a computer. Some will use a projector and screen as if presenting to any in-person group. Others will use a green screen using their logo as a backdrop. Whether you use a camera on a stage or your computer at your office, presenting while standing and engaging the group will make your presentation more memorable and persuasive.

The slides are not the show. Your virtual presentation isn't just the slides on Zoom, Webex, and Join.Me. You are the message. No matter what your virtual platform, always make sure that you are the show. Slides are merely there to serve as illustrations and reminders. But slides are not the focus. Prospects buy you, not the images. They buy rapport and trust with you. The more that's remembered, the higher your closing ratio.

When to Send Supporting Materials

As always, it's a good idea to send supporting materials before your virtual presentation as well as after. An example of information you can send ahead of time could be an agenda, perhaps your bio, the company brochure, and even testimonials. Send these by email to attendees and clients/prospects. Many platforms will allow you to make your presentation downloadable to the attendees. This solves the problem of attendees not receiving the emailed presentation.

In rank order, the first item you should send is the agenda. It's important that the prospect have a reason to meet. All the other information is supportive. I discussed earlier about recording a three-minute demo introducing yourself and what you plan to discuss at the meeting. This is a wonderful idea but also needs to be supplemented by written information sent ahead of the meeting.

After the meeting, it's important to follow up with a summary of what was discussed. But this is also where you might get in trouble. A brief executive summary will go a lot further than a boilerplate follow-up message. For example, an introductory sentence might be, "It was great meeting and talking to you on Tuesday." You can then follow this with three bullet points discussed during the virtual meeting. Then you can include a follow-up plan with the date of the next virtual conference. Anything else you put in the follow-up could be supporting materials. But it will be rare that anybody will read more than a few paragraphs on the first page.

One rule of thumb is to send written materials before meeting with existing clients. But only send materials after a virtual meeting with new prospects. The reason is that clients have already bought from you and only want to know the price as a detail to consider. New prospects will read any materials you send and be distracted by pricing information. New prospects are often more likely to disqualify you than to find a reason to buy. Existing clients are more likely to find a reason to buy than to disqualify. Clients already decided to buy. Prospects have not yet made that decision.

5

Virtual Events and Webinars

Whether you are in real estate, financial planning, mortgage sales, or even network marketing, producing and conducting a successful webinar will dramatically increase your sales and income. Virtual events can be highly successful or, if done poorly, a money pit.

One of the most frequent questions I have received in the last couple of years is how to get more engagement during virtual webinars. Many of my coaching clients use them to get leads. During the pandemic, webinars would replace in-person seminars as a way to prospect fifty potential buyers/clients in the time it takes to get one.

Many salespeople in the retirement sales community habitually held dinner seminars. Many in the real estate investment industry conducted evening events to attract prospects. These topics could be how to buy a property effectively, flip a house, and even how to negotiate a good deal. I know about lead-generation seminars because I have been the guest speaker at many. Some companies elect to do webinars discussing products or services. But they need a guest author/guest speaker to attract a bigger audience. Often at retirement seminars, the speech topic would be my book *Why Smart People Make Dumb Mistakes with their Money.*

During and soon after COVID-19, webinars became the only way to get in front of groups of people. Nobody would come to in-person events. The problem with booking appointments at webinars is engagement.

The rule of thumb for any in-person event is to expect 25 percent not to be qualified. Another 25 percent will come only for something free such as the dinner. That leaves just 50 percent who are qualified and interested. Among them, half are likely to book an appointment with the presenter. If you put all that altogether, only five attendees out of twenty will book an appointment. Among the five, only three will show up. These numbers reflect the results of an in-person dinner seminar, not a virtual event.

A virtual presentation unfortunately generates even worse results. Let's say a presenter advertises on Facebook to get attendees to a seminar. That financial advisor, for example, is likely to get about ten to attend. Possibly two will book appointments, and both are likely to cancel. The same presenter will spend nearly $3,000 in marketing costs for $0 return. These marketing companies will advertise to thousands of social media platforms netting only a few attendees. The cost to put on a virtual meeting on any platform is minor. But the third-party marketing costs could be substantial. Most will learn a lesson and never do another.

I spoke to one coaching candidate who was sure he would get twenty attendees at a virtual webinar. I told him the response numbers were based on industry statistics. He completely disagreed and said he had a better way of getting people to attend and a much more effective way to book appointments. I checked in two weeks after the webinar. He had fifteen attendees and booked five appointments in which all five canceled. Sure enough, he had spent $3,000 for no benefit.

Virtual presentations and webinars are tough ways to generate leads. While face-to-face meetings are likely to at least break even, you can lose a lot of money doing a webinar. Most of the webinars where I speak as a guest are populated by existing groups who meet regularly. I may speak to a company or association that meets quarterly or annually. Perhaps an association will use me to speak at their virtual convention.

In this chapter I'll tell you about putting together your own webinar as well as speaking at a meeting that is already organized. You could be the presenter at a planned meeting or produce your own. Both will result in more sales. I will discuss how to organize your webinar using a systematic approach in presenting your ideas, how to book appointments, and even how to make those appointments stick.

How to Become a Great Presenter

I spoke many years ago to a huge group of a thousand in Las Vegas. I got a standing ovation, which is always a good feeling. Coincidentally, the speaker after me actually presented on How to Speak in Front of Groups. The first thing he said to the big audience was, "Most Americans have three fears. Number one is speaking in front of a group. Number two is dying. Number three is dying while speaking in front of a group." I laughed until my stomach hurt. It was so descriptive.

Most of us are terrified to speak in front of an audience. The rest of us are so self-conscious that we become robotic and lose spontaneity. Perhaps the most important advice is to stay calm. Here are a few ideas to help you relax during any presentation, let alone at a webinar.

PRACTICE FIVE TIMES OUT LOUD.

Most of us will write out a speech. You may be tempted to deliver the speech as written. It may seem logical since you are probably a subject matter expert. But there's a big difference between your speech on paper and presenting it. You need to accentuate certain areas. You need to wait for the audience to respond. You need to engage them with examples and stories. You also need to learn how to time each area of the speech.

The virtual speech is by nature of the medium impersonal. It is hard to engage more than a few attendees. A virtual attendee can just walk away from the presentation, mute themselves, or even leave when the event fails to hold their interest. Recently, my daughter Stacey played a round of golf with me while logged on to a virtual event. Since the presenters didn't engage the attendees, the host never knew who was engaged and who was playing golf.

Every presentation skill discussed is applicable not only in a virtual environment but also in a face-to-face venue. One other issue is the audience's resistance to interact. You are less likely to see them clap when they agree or laugh at humor. Audiences also respond more when they see other attendees respond. When they are alone, there is more of a resistance to respond. The unfortunate byproduct is that the more a group responds, the better the presenter performs. Just like a tennis player who is pumped by the cheers of a crowd, a presenter will become more engaging and fun if the audience looks like they are engaged.

You can't do all that without rehearsing out loud. There is a huge difference between knowing your topic and delivering it to a hundred people. The best way to become comfortable in delivering a presentation is to do it out loud at least five times.

I would love to say I practice what I preach. I try. But rehearsing is always a struggle. I hate to practice speeches. I was taught to practice in front of a mirror. The idea from a Toastmasters instructor was that if I could see my own face during the speech, I could also see what the audience sees. Sometimes, I would go in the backyard of my house and find a quiet space. Practice never came naturally. I'm nothing as a speaker without the inspiration of an audience.

My compromise was to practice speeches during drive time. This actually worked out well since I really can't read a speech while driving. I would put speech notes on the console to the right of the steering wheel. But since I was driving, I could only glance at keywords. These keywords would be highlighted in yellow and even underlined. This was good practice for the real thing since, during any speech, you only have time to glance at your notes, noticing keywords and memory joggers. You obviously only want to glance at your notes since reading or spending time looking at your notes would be as dangerous as driving while texting.

I would often practice while traveling to a conference. But since I always wanted the presentation to be natural, I would rehearse while driving a rental car to a resort. Or I would talk to myself on a veranda outside a hotel room. My wife would usually get a chuckle watching me through the glass slider motioning with my hands and pointing as if I had PowerPoint slides to reference. But it worked.

The helpful part about practicing out loud is that you can hear yourself. You can learn where the stories should be inserted. You can get a feeling as to where to insert humor. As you do the presentation out loud, you can hear yourself. If you can avoid reading the speech, you will focus more on the audience.

RELAX.

A wonderful way to become comfortable is to know exactly what to say. Learning the presentation inside and out will give you confidence and comfort. But there are times when the anxiety makes you self-conscious. When stress gets high enough, you may feel stage fright.

Stage fright is surprisingly common even among stage professionals. Twenty-five percent of performers suffer stage fright to some extent. If you are part of an orchestra or a band, the anxiety may be diminished since you can hide behind your fellow performers. The Beatles drummer, Ringo Starr, was said to have debilitating stage fright. He insisted on being somewhat hidden behind the rest of the group. It was only many years later that he was willing to sing solos.

Stage fright dissipates with experience. But it rarely goes away completely. Perhaps the most difficult performance is a solo act.

My biggest audience was 26,000 at the MGM Grand in Las Vegas. I was the keynote speaker for RE/MAX real estate and followed Stuart Varney, a cable news host. Varney spoke behind a podium and read his speech. After a few introductory comments, I walked to the middle of the stage far from the podium. I have been speaking to audiences since 1981. The most relaxed I get on stage is when I can physically engage with attendees.

That day in front of 26,000, I walked down from the eight-foot stage into the front row. There were three camera crews following me as I walked through the crowd. No speaker had ever done that with such a large group. But it was the only way that I could stay relaxed. It also turned out to be a perfect way to engage all 26,000.

Whether you are speaking to 26,000 in person or ten people on a virtual call, you need to relax. When you aren't comfortable, you may focus more on how you feel than on how the audience is receiving the material. When you can get comfortable with the group you are addressing, your presentation will be better received.

How to Eliminate Stage Fright

Most with stage fright simply avoid speaking in front of groups. But if you are one of the 25 percent or more who find speaking to groups debilitating, here are a few tips that you can use right now. Anxiety doesn't just occur when speaking to 26,000. It can also diminish your performance presenting to only five at a virtual webinar.

Discuss your fear with your physician who might recommend a prescription medication or an over-the-counter supplement to calm your situational anxiety. You'll want to discuss any adverse reactions or contraindications that may occur with any substances, and of course try them well before the day of your presentation to see how you react.

MEASURING ANXIETY

A scale developed by psychiatrist Joseph Wolpe illustrates how anxiety affects you. This scale is called the Subjective Unit of Discomfort Scale (SUDS).

SUDS 0 to 40

This measurement interval shows the amount of anxiety you might have as you wake up in the morning. You may become more alert as you drink that first cup of coffee. Your anxiety level may increase as you stretch in the morning. SUDS may also increase after taking a shower and becoming more alert.

SUDS 40 to 60

This is what Joseph Wolpe called peak performance. Anxiety and stress can actually help you perform better. If there isn't enough stress, we feel sluggish and groggy. But with too much stress, we feel irritable, lose memory, and have poor emotional control. We may even become agitated. The trick is to keep yourself in the 40 to 60 range.

SUDS 60 to 100

This is the burnout area. Over 60 on the SUDS scale is when anxiety and stress become debilitating. You feel like a truck hit you at the end of the day. Headaches are pronounced. All you want to do is relax. You may go to your favorite bar on the way home. You may want to de-stress by watching TV, avoiding having to think.

The trick is to never let yourself get above 60. When your SUDS increases above 60 during a presentation, either on a virtual webinar or in front of an audience, you will feel anxiety and stage fright.

PROGRESSIVE RELAXATION

One answer to decreasing SUDS is to imagine yourself sitting in a chair. First, tighten up muscle groups and relax them as you decrease anxiety levels. While you are sitting, tense up your head and neck muscles for five seconds and relax. Then tense up your shoulders, chest, and upper back for five seconds and relax. Tense up each muscle group this way all the way down your body to your toes.

Once you have done the muscle tightening and relaxation exercise, imagine yourself at the top of a staircase walking down one step at a time. With every step, you will take a breath in and a breath out in a long exhale. At the bottom of the ten steps, imagine yourself in a relaxing place. It can be on an empty beach or lying on a blanket under a tree on a warm day. Stay in that relaxing place for about five minutes. Your legs should be tingling. Your heart rate and breathing should slow. Eventually you will relax so much you will nearly fall asleep. Your SUDS level will drop dramatically.

Progressive relaxation will help you become more calm and comfortable during any presentation. It's a good idea to practice this for a week before your presentation. Then an hour before to bring your SUDS level down. Often SUDS is highest immediately before your presentation. For many presenters, SUDS will decrease as the presentation goes on. But for others, if SUDS is too high, it will only continue to diminish your performance.

Some of my clients feel more comfortable during an in-person event. While others are more relaxed in a virtual setting. But in a post-COVID world, you need to be comfortable in both settings—virtual and in person.

ANCHORING RELAXATION

At the point of greatest relaxation, fold your arms. Or put your hands on your hips. This is a technique called anchoring. You can use this during presentations at your home office or anywhere else to relax yourself whenever you sense SUDS increasing above 60. For example, after you have practiced folding your arms, or placed your hands on hips a few times, you should bring yourself to a peak relaxation level or SUDS between 40 to 60.

You can do anchoring anytime. The more you practice this, the bigger and more immediate the impact. You should practice enough to relax anytime you feel an anxiety increase. Let's test out the anchor's effectiveness now. Try to get a sense of where your SUDS level is. Think of a SUDS score that best represents your anxiety right now. We will see if we can decrease that level. Just as you earlier put hands on your hips while on the beach or under the tree, do it again right now. Whether you folded your arms while under the imaginary tree or on the beach, do that anchor again right now.

Did your SUDS level decrease? Practice this five times. Anytime you feel your SUDS level increasing, you can use anchoring to relax. When you get good at this, you can drive anxiety levels down anytime you want.

Most psychotherapists recommend slow exhales during periods of anxiety. When stressed, we tend to breathe quickly to the point of shortness of breath. If you can exhale slowly, the anxiety will dissipate also. But a much better technique to decrease anxiety and SUDS is to use anchoring.

If you are in the middle of a webinar and feel your SUDS level and anxiety increase, it's difficult to exhale slowly while speaking during the presentation. But using an anchor will look totally natural to the audience. This will work whether you're speaking to a group of 26,000 or doing a webinar for five.

Since anxiety, stress, and stage fright are so common during any kind of presentation, virtual or not, most people will avoid speaking unless they have to. But your ability to speak to groups may be the single best way to increase sales and build your expertise. Don't avoid public speaking because of stress. Embrace it and channel stage fright by using the techniques I discussed.

How to Deliver Riveting Presentations

Let's face it. Most presenters are boring. They talk too long and aren't particularly interesting. Often the message isn't relevant or presented in a way that captures attention. Professional speakers use certain tricks, whether the presentation is a virtual webinar or a Zoom meeting for three, to make their messages riveting, memorable, and engaging.

As discussed earlier, when presenting a sales solution to prospects or clients use the 333 strategy when delivering a virtual presentation. But if you are presenting to a group in a webinar or nonsales environment, you have more time. If your webinar is only twenty minutes, don't present more than three concepts. But in a longer format such as a ninety-minute workshop, you can present up to five concepts at a sitting. Whether you speak at a webinar or to a large group, structure is critical.

Never present more than five concepts at any one sitting. Most novice speakers make two basic mistakes. They either present too much information in a confusing way or don't present enough applicable information, glossing over a topic. If you broke your presentation into five parts, what would they be? For example, if your presentation was on retirement planning, you might discuss these five topics:

1. Running out of money during retirement
2. Market volatility
3. Taxes
4. Inflation
5. Family legacy

If your topic is real estate investing, what five subjects would you include? If your message is network marketing, what would be your five topics?

If you limit your presentation to five concepts, you would first tease them in your agenda at the beginning of the talk. At the end of the presentation, you could summarize the five concepts you spoke about. The most important advice is to stay organized and structured.

You and I have both heard far too many rambling speakers. You have heard that if an attendee can get one idea out of a presentation, it's a success. That slogan is shortsighted. You ought to be able to get five. If you can't remember five things a speaker presents, even one day after a speech, it wasn't well organized and presented. Based on our studies on the focal screen, attendees will remember 3+/-2 concepts. Even three would be an improvement over one.

Let's test this concept out. Ask a friend or colleague to do an experiment with you. Read ten, two-digit numbers to them slowly over ten full seconds. Tell them before the exercise that they can't write the numbers down and even have to count down out loud from 100 to 95 after you read the numbers. To make this exercise easier, here are the steps:

A: "I am going to read you ten numbers. You can't write them down, only listen and try to recall later how many you remember."
22   35   67   26   83   91   52   43   74   61

B: "Now count back from 100 with me out loud so you can't verbally rehearse the numbers."
100, 99, 98, 97, 96, 95 . . .

C: "Okay, how many numbers do you recall? Say them."

There are a few outcomes that result from this exercise. One is that your participant will recall 3+/–2 numbers. The other is that they will recall only the first few and the last few. This is the primacy recency effect. This means your webinar or virtual sales participant will only recall what they first hear and what they last hear. The obvious recommendation is to present an agenda or overview in the beginning and a review at the end. This will go a long way to ensuring your listener will remember more of what they hear.

The Five-Step Process

Besides limiting a presentation to five concepts, effective speakers are skilled at keeping audiences attentive and engaged. There is no difference whether you are delivering a virtual or in-person presentation. All these steps apply. In fact because of the lack of face-to-face engagement, there is perhaps a greater need on a virtual platform to present effectively.

Here are five ways to keep the attention of any audience at any time. This five-step process can be used in any group presentation. Remember to present only five concepts at a single sitting.

1. ASK A RHETORICAL QUESTION.

The best speakers always ask a question at the beginning of a message. They hurt and rescue. They ask if anybody has experienced a particular dilemma or problem. This suggests the speaker will have the answer. For example, a rhetorical question could be, "Have you ever wondered whether your money may last as long as you do?" Or a real estate–based rhetorical question might be, "How many of you would like to make $30,000 more per property flip?" If you know your audience and their concerns, a rhetorical question in the beginning of the sequence will be riveting. The rhetorical question suggests a promise to the audience that you will solve a problem.

2. MAKE YOUR POINT.

This is the answer to that rhetorical question. You are providing expertise in solving the audience's concern. It could be showing the attendees how they can make their retirement investments last thirty years with portfolio diversification. It could even be showing how an annuity could provide income without losses due to market volatility. If your rhetorical question is about increasing profits in flipping properties, one point could be how to negotiate a lower sales price. You could also talk about the five areas to spend remodeling money in building the most return on the property investment.

3. ILLUSTRATE YOUR POINT.

Do this with statistics, quotes, and data. Often illustrations are more eye-opening than the actual points you make. When I illustrate a concept, my favorite method is to discuss the research behind it. Often, the psychological research and how it is done is more entertaining than the point itself.

Ellen Langer, a Harvard researcher, discovered that the word *because* gained more compliance than any other word. Using the word *because* in combination with any request will work. But the illustration is more fun. College researchers asked a woman to cut in line to make photocopies. You can imagine how long ago this was if they stood in line at a copier.

Asking to cut in line achieved only 17 percent compliance. The researchers then told the young woman to cut in line saying she had a deadline. That excuse achieved an 83 percent compliance. One enterprising researcher wondered if it was the reason she used to cut in line, or was it simply the use of the word *because*. She was instructed to say *because* but also gave an obvious statement at the end. She said, "Do you mind if I cut in line to make some photocopies *because* I need to make some photocopies." The acceptance ratio of 83 percent was maintained. Acquiescence was due solely to the use of the word *because*. This is a good example of how the illustration can actually be more entertaining than the point you're making.

4. APPLY THE POINT.

The most important part of the sequence is how the point can apply to the listener. It's one thing to hear an interesting concept. But when you can show the listener how they can apply it, everybody on the virtual call or presentation will become more attentive.

The best way to apply any point is to use a story. Stories sell, facts tell. The most important goal of any speaker is to get the listener motivated enough to act on the message. A concept is interesting. An illustration and application of the concept can be entertaining. But a story can change someone's heart as well as inspire and motivate. The strongest memories I have of any concept are related to how well I remember the story illustrating it.

In 1981, I was a stockbroker with Kidder-Peabody, a wire-house brokerage selling securities. I moved to Orange County, California, from San Diego to join the company. Soon after, I met Dennis Renter. Dennis was a few years older than I and coincidentally also in the financial planning business. A tennis player, he and I became fast friends and are close even today. After our first match, Dennis asked about my goals. I told him I wanted to buy a boat and rent a mooring in Newport Harbor, California. I was all of twenty-five years old. Dennis knew that going in debt at such an early age would be the stupidest thing possible for someone starting out.

He told me about a concept called dollar cost averaging. This is a way to put a small amount of money away consistently using the wealth building process of compounding. Albert Einstein once said compounding is the eighth wonder of the world. I ignored Dennis and thought about asking somebody else for a recommendation for a loan. At that point, Dennis pulled out six pictures of a client who did dollar cost averaging investment for four years. He was able to save and buy a beautiful Swan fifty-two-foot sloop-rigged sailboat. This was and is the Rolls Royce of sailboats.

The family dollar-cost-averaged for four years accumulating $400,000 for the boat and was even able to finance a two-year journey sailing throughout the South Pacific. As Dennis described the investment plan, he showed me pictures of the family barbecuing on the back of the boat at sunset. He displayed pictures of the dad in scuba gear, scraping barnacles off the bottom of the boat. One picture showed the boat heeling over in a strong wind. The family obviously enjoyed every minute.

With every picture, I became more persuaded that dollar cost averaging was exactly what I needed to do. To this day, I remember the concept because of the sailboat story. When you use memorable stories to apply concepts, you will be able to motivate anyone, no matter what the forum or platform. Whether it's a virtual speech, webinar, or even an in-person presentation to 26,000, everyone who hears you will be influenced and hopefully motivated.

5. SEGUE TO THE NEXT FIVE-STEP SEQUENCE.

The last part is to segue to the next five-step process. This could be a one-liner, quick story, or even audience participation.

One of my speeches is titled *How to Read Your Client's Mind.* The first concept I talk about is how to increase persuasion and memory by touching somebody briefly on the arm. Research has shown that if you want someone to remember a concept, touch them on the arm less than three seconds while you talk about it. Memory and retention of that idea will go up by 83 percent versus not touching.

Once I make the point to touch someone, I illustrate the concept with research. I apply it by asking all audience members to physically touch the person next to them and say something nice. It takes some cajoling, but everyone participates. Not only does the audience learn the concept, but they also experience it physically. But the segue to the following concept is the most fun.

Many years ago, I spoke to the Million Dollar Round Table meeting in Vancouver, British Columbia. The day after my presentation, an attendee walked up as I was signing books. He said, "That touching below the elbow thing really works!" I asked how he knew. He had walked into Cardrena's restaurant near the convention center the evening after I spoke. A server was standing with a tray of tequila shooters. She had no luck selling the drinks.

The attendee asked, "Are you having problems selling tequila tonight?"

She said, "Yes, nobody likes tequila. I think it's just a bad economy. Nobody can afford it."

He said, "I just heard a speaker today who might help. Why don't you walk up to the guy in the corner, touch him below the elbow briefly, and ask if he wants to buy a shooter."

She said, "I'm not going to walk up to a stranger and touch him."

The attendee said, "Nothing else is working. Why don't you try it?"

She approached the closest customer, tapped him on the arm below the elbow and said, "Would you like to buy tequila for yourself or a tray for the whole table?"

All the drinks were sold in ten minutes. She put her tray down and walked over to stare out of a bayfront window, and the attendee asked, "Did it work?"

She said, "Yes, really well."

He said, "Why don't you get another tray?"

And she said, "I don't want to do that anymore. It worked too well. I think it's unethical!"

A segue that's both an illustration as well as a cute story can perfectly set up the next five-step sequence. When you can get participation during a speech, as well as use a story of how somebody applied your concept, you can change lives. You will become much more persuasive and motivating in everything you present. Remember to never present more than five concepts at any one sitting. But when you present any concept, use the five steps. Include stories to gain emotion and influence. Nothing else can persuade like a great story.

In a virtual setting, you can't get the same kind of physical audience participation. But you can get attendees to interact. Using the example earlier remembering ten numbers, you can tell the audience you will recite ten numbers and then call on someone in the meeting at random to recall as many as they can. You can also ask attendees to write down a response to a question. Be as creative as possible. The point is to engage the virtual audience.

Virtual Limits on Presentation Attention

One of the biggest differences in a virtual versus face-to-face event is the amount of time the attendee will pay attention. When you are face-to-face, the maximum attention is about ninety minutes. Often meeting planners ask me to speak for two hours. I usually agree as long as there is a ten-minute break in the middle. Even the most brilliant speakers can only keep an audience's attention for ninety minutes. The mind can only focus on what the rear end (and bladder) can endure.

Virtual events are different. There is a much shorter attention span. You will never retain a group's focus more than forty-five minutes. In fact, your goal should be thirty minutes allowing a fifteen-minute float in case the meeting goes long. I have done webinars, small virtual meetings, and face-to-face keynote addresses for more than forty years. I did my first Webex seminar about twenty-five years ago. Computers were slow and connecting to the conference platform was a challenge. Back then we used a telephone line to connect to the internet.

But then, like now, I always pay close attention to when attendees start dropping off any webinar. It is always forty-five minutes or slightly earlier. Perhaps some of my presentations commanded attention longer. But then some of my presentations weren't as interesting. The virtual presentation barrier always seems to be about forty-five minutes.

During physical seminars at hotel conference rooms, there may be no place for an attendee to go. They may just stay in the meeting room reading their cell phone text messages during a speech. But a virtual webinar is different. They will just disconnect from the meeting. Unless they are getting continuing education credit, the attendee count can go from one hundred to twenty in no time (most webinar platforms show you the number of attendees).

The rule of thumb in presenting at a webinar is to never speak more than forty-five minutes. When you do a virtual presentation to a small group of two or three, your time limit will be even less—about twenty minutes. It doesn't matter whether you're a real estate agent doing a virtual home tour, a car sales rep virtually showing vehicles on a lot, or even a rep demonstrating software, your limit is twenty minutes. If you use tie-downs and trial closes, you may be able to build in an extra ten minutes. But if you fail to engage your attendees, you may only get ten minutes of attention before they check out.

When I do a webinar for even a group of fifty, I engage attendees every five minutes. Sometimes my questions will be rhetorical. Other times, I will ask and wait for an answer. But generally, I will brief five of the attendees before the meeting and let them know I may call on them sometime during the presentation. I don't want them to leave the meeting to get a cup of coffee or take a bathroom break. The awkward silence while you wait is even more pronounced on a virtual call. Sometimes silence after I call someone's name can be humorous in itself. Johnny Carson, thirty years ago on the *Tonight Show*, always had a funny line to follow a joke that fell flat.

How to Book Appointments at Virtual Events

One of the hardest tasks to do at a webinar, or any other large virtual event, is to book appointments that stick. There are many reasons why this is so difficult. One is the lack of engagement. Often attendees can hide behind their computers because they aren't as involved as they would be in person. Another reason is that the topic is not interesting enough or doesn't have an application useful enough to the attendee.

The biggest reason why appointments are challenging to book at virtual events is emotional engagement. Whether the meeting is on retirement planning, real estate, network marketing, or even a new software application, the best time to book an appointment is during the event, not after. Many speakers will send a follow-up email pitching a product or offering an appointment. The response to these emails is minimal. Other more enterprising organizers will try to call attendees a few days after the meeting. It often takes three to five dials over a few days to get an attendee on the phone. By that time, audiences barely remember the points that were presented, let alone they were even there.

I've mentioned a lot in this book about memory and retention. According to research conducted during my graduate days at UCSD, we forget 70 percent of what we hear within twenty-four hours and 90 percent after three days. If you wait a few days to try to book an appointment over the phone, the attendee will barely remember anything. By the time they answer the phone, they are unlikely to book an appointment to find out more.

Here are a couple of ideas that will help you book appointments and make them stick. At the very end of an event, get attendees to rate their interest. For example, on a 1 to 5 scale, 1 could be no interest, while a 5 is an area of great concern. If you were doing a retirement seminar, you would ask the question, "Are you concerned about running out of money during retirement?" After you ask a question, you would ask the attendees to mark a 1 if they are not concerned, or a 5 if they are very concerned. They could also mark down any number in the middle.

The second question could be market volatility. You might ask them to rate their response to, "I'm concerned about losing my money during retirement." You then would tell them to mark 1 if they are unconcerned or 5 if they are very concerned. Or 2 to 4 if they didn't feel strongly either way.

At the end of these questions, you could ask the attendees to respond if they marked 3 or higher for any one of the questions.

While 35 percent will mark 5 on individual questions, 90 percent will have marked 3 or higher on at least one. Anyone who marked a question 3 or higher would be asked to mark the box below that states, "Yes, I would like to book an appointment."

Many of my clients will add in possible appointment dates and times at the bottom of the rating sheet. The attendee can indicate their first appointment choice of time and date and also a possible second date. If you are doing an in-person dinner seminar, it would be easy to incentivize the group to turn the sheets in. You would simply offer to put each response sheet in a raffle for a dinner for two at an upscale restaurant. The only way they could enter the raffle is to turn in a sheet.

Getting response sheets is more difficult in a virtual environment. But there are still a few ways to do this. One is to send the response sheets to attendees before the event as a downloadable PDF. Once they complete them, the attendees can scan and email the sheets back. One way to do this is to offer to put those who send sheets back into a raffle for a free dinner for two, as long as they send the sheet back before the event.

The Zoom platform has a utility that allows attendees to answer questions and surveys while they are on the webinar. On Zoom, it is called polling. All you have to do is set up the polling questions and present them at the appropriate time. Zoom will even save the answers through a downloadable spreadsheet you can review later. Through this polling utility, you can pick a raffle winner who responded to the questions. This solves the problem of waiting until after the webinar to get the sheets returned.

Here is an example of how some of my financial clients use rating sheets. It will be easy to apply this concept to your industry. This sheet will give you an idea of how to structure the attendee responses. You can use the self-rating system of booking appointments in any industry. If you did a webinar on how to flip real

---

"Client Family & Friend Dinner Party" Summit House Restaurant March 8	FINANCIAL STRATEGIES for Today and Tomorrow Wealth Management Group a Registered Investment Advisory Firm

Name: _____

Day Phone: (_____) _____-_____   Evening Phone: (_____) _____-_____
Cell Phone: (_____) _____-_____   E-Mail: _____
Address _____
City, State, Zip _____

*We hold this information in strict confidence, and we do not give, rent, or sell such information to anyone

---

How Did We Do?

How informative was the workshop? _____ Very   _____ Somewhat   _____ None

---

On a scale of 1-5, how much does each topic below concern you? Circle your response below.
1= Not a Concern   5 = Urgent Concern

☐	Running out of money during retirement (Outliving Investments)	1 2 3 4 5
☐	Investment volatility (The risk of losing my investment dollars)	1 2 3 4 5
☐	Decreasing taxes during retirement (Income or Estate Tax)	1 2 3 4 5
☐	Leaving a Family Legacy (Protecting my beneficiaries' inheritance)	1 2 3 4 5
☐	Cost of catastrophic illness (Spending my savings on a Nursing Home Stay)	1 2 3 4 5

For your complimentary meeting, please indicate your *1st and 2nd choice* next to a time slot.

Friday, March 9	Monday, March 12	Tuesday, March 13	Wednesday, March 14
9:00 AM FILLED	9:00 AM _____	9:00 AM _____	9:00 AM _____
11:00 AM FILLED	11:00 AM _____	11:00 AM _____	11:00 AM _____
1:00 PM _____	1:00 PM _____	1:00 PM _____	1:00 PM FILLED
3:00 PM _____	3:00 PM _____	3:00 PM FILLED	3:00 PM _____
5:00 PM FILLED	5:00 PM _____	5:00 PM FILLED	5:00 PM FILLED

Thursday, March 15	Friday, March 16	Monday, March 19	Tuesday, March 20
9:00 AM FILLED	9:00 AM FILLED	9:00 AM FILLED	9:00 AM FILLED
11:00 AM _____	11:00 AM _____	11:00 AM FILLED	11:00 AM _____
1:00 PM _____	1:00 PM _____	1:00 PM _____	1:00 PM _____
3:00 PM _____	3:00 PM _____	3:00 PM _____	3:00 PM _____
5:00 PM _____	5:00 PM FILLED	5:00 PM _____	5:00 PM _____

I am still working and I can only see you in the evening.

Monday   Tuesday   Wednesday   Thursday
(Please circle best evenings)

estate properties, just create five questions and ask the attendees rate their concerns 1 to 5. If you did a webinar on network marketing, you could use the same method of asking five questions to get the attendees to again rate their concerns.

Making Appointments Stick

Booking an appointment is tough. Making sure people show up is sometimes impossible. The industry average is 35 percent will book an appointment and 25 percent won't show up. If you have a small webinar with fifteen people, five might book appointments and two might show up. You better hope those two buy; otherwise, you could lose thousands of dollars in marketing expenses. But if every appointment you booked showed up and was even excited to talk to you, would that help?

Here comes the magic. This is the secret sauce. Call all attendees who booked appointments and filled out a rating sheet. You should first reference the webinar and ask what they liked. But instead of trying to immediately confirm the appointment, you will instead ask them about any concerns rated 3 or higher.

For example, you might open with this: "I notice you marked down 3 on the question regarding running out of money. Why did you rate it a 3?" Think of the power you will have in reminding the attendee of their highly rated concerns and the reason they marked the score. They will not deny their answers on the sheet. You are only reminding them. They will tell you a lot more than just the score.

Let me introduce you to the Five-Step Bridge:

1. Introductory sentence
2. Search for needs
3. Recap
4. Trial close
5. Book an appointment

Here's a sample conversation of how to incorporate the Five-Step Bridge in an attendee appointment follow-up call.

1. INTRODUCTORY SENTENCE

REP: "Hi, Mr. Smith. This is Kerry Johnson from Johnson Financial. You attended our webinar last Monday on retirement planning. Do you remember the webinar?"

2. SEARCH FOR NEEDS

REP: "I noticed that you marked down a 4 for running out of money. What was your thought behind that score?"

ATTENDEE: "Well, my mom is nearly ninety and completely dependent on me for income. I don't want to end up dependent on my own kids in retirement. That's really important to me."

REP: "I also noticed that you marked down a 5 for taxes during retirement. What was your thought behind that?"

ATTENDEE: "Taxes almost never go down. Most of these politicians look at retirement accounts and think it's their own piggy bank. I want to make sure that taxes don't take too big of a bite out of my retirement."

REP: "Lastly, I noticed that you marked a 5 for family legacy. Why did you give it that score?"

ATTENDEE: "I had to put myself through college by working all four years. It was really difficult. I had barely enough time to study and certainly had no time for friends. I want my grandkids to be able to study and get good grades without worrying about money. I want to pay their tuition so they can enjoy their college experience. That's really important to me."

3. RECAP

REP: "So if I heard you correctly, you don't want to run out of money and be dependent on your children for retirement. You also believe that taxes will go up and that you don't want the government to take a bite out of your retirement account. And you want to provide college tuition for your grandkids so they can get good grades and not have to worry about money. Did I get all that right?"

ATTENDEE: "Yes, that's exactly right. I want to do all those things in retirement."

4. TRIAL CLOSE

REP: "If we could take a look at making sure that you're not dependent on your kids during retirement, make sure the government doesn't take a bite out of your retirement account, and prevent your grandkids from worrying about money during college, with that be helpful?"

ATTENDEE: "Yes I would love that."

5. BOOK AN APPOINTMENT

REP: "I have you down for Tuesday at ten o'clock in the
morning. Is this still a good time for you?"

ATTENDEE: "Yes that sounds great. I will see you there at ten
o'clock."

Does it make sense that if you follow this system, not only will you book appointments, but your prospects will show up? People only cancel appointments when they don't value or remember the reason for scheduling it in the first place. They can't remember the event or what was said.

But with this webinar appointment system, you can motivate attendees to self-rate their concerns. Based on a score of 3 or higher, you can inspire them to book an appointment. You can incentivize them to return the response sheets by conducting a raffle for an attractive prize.

But here's the best part. They will answer your phone calls. Since they forgot everything at your meeting, you can remind them of their responses and ask why they marked each question the score they did. Then recap their concerns like a good psycho-therapist. You can ask if those concerns are still valid. Next, you can trial-close to make sure they are committed to finding solutions. Again, they will say yes. And finally you can confirm the appointment already marked on the sheet. The best part is that they remember why they booked the appointment and will be enthusiastic about meeting with you.

How to Book Appointments with Disinterested Attendees

Sometimes you will get rating sheets back with lower scores of 1 and 2. These folks do not seem to be concerned enough to book an appointment. First, let's assume you did a virtual event or webinar without using the rating sheet and want to follow up. What would you say on the phone? "Did you like the webinar?" "Do you want to book an appointment?" Almost nobody would take you up because they can't remember the event. If they can't remember the event, why would they book an appointment?

But what if you had their rating sheet? What if you asked them about the question marked 2 and still did the Five-Step Bridge? You would still get them to talk. They may give the five questions a second thought. Perhaps they mismarked the answers. Perhaps they are more concerned now. It will never be a wasted call since you will resist pitching an appointment. You now have the Five-Step Bridge. No attendee will reject you again.

This is the most elegant and effective appointment booking system available. It doesn't matter if you are doing a webinar on real estate, accounting, or underwater soap carving, this system will work. All you have to do is get creative and discover which questions to use on the survey. The 1 to 5 rating system will work no matter the topic. Using this system will book at least 65 percent of the attendees into appointments. Your cancellation rate will be minimal because each attendee will remember why they are meeting with you. Use the five-step appointment rating system from now on. You are spending enormous amounts of money attracting attendees to your virtual events or webinars. Why not book as many high-quality appointments as possible? You can even use this system in a face-to-face in-person event. It will be even more effective because it will be easier to get the response sheets back.

6

Using Social Media
to Sell Virtually

t is impossible to talk about virtual sales without also discussing social media—an important part of any lead-generation strategy. If you are business-to-business, LinkedIn is the go-to platform. If consumers are your target market, Facebook is likely the best place to be. Twitter is a quick way to communicate with followers, but engagement can be limited.

I'm a business-to-business speaker and author. Nearly all my clients come from referrals. Therefore, LinkedIn is absolutely the best source of new business and branding for me. There are several ways to use LinkedIn as well as any other social media platform. First is to build your brand.

The father of modern-day advertising, John Wanamaker, once said, "50 percent of advertising doesn't work. I just don't know which half that is." You can spend enormous amounts of money on advertising. It is often a money pit. You can also be diligent about the money you spend. It all depends on the message and how you target a market. If your message is right, but targets the wrong audience, resources will be wasted. If your target is right with the wrong message, the same will happen.

An entrepreneur spent millions producing a dog food blend of healthy ingredients so nourishing that it could extend any dog's life. It promised to include probiotics, help the dog's hair shine, and calm down anxiety. But sales never took off. The president called in the sales force and demanded to know why they weren't producing business. They simply said, "The dogs won't eat it." We need to have the right dog food as well as reach owners who want it.

The Two Types of Advertising

Direct response advertising is an attempt to advertise by getting prospects to contact you. It may entail making an offer. You want the recipient so compelled that they respond with questions or even decide to buy on the spot. Examples are commercials that run on late-night cable TV. Also, most ads on Facebook are direct response. These ads often offer 10 to 20 percent discounts. They may also include a time limit to get you to respond now.

Sometimes advertisers try to motivate by showing a five-minute countdown clock in the corner of the infomercial screen. I'm not sure it fools anybody. If you buy one minute after the deadline, would the advertiser insist you missed the cutoff time?

Branding is a second type of advertising. If you can build a brand, you can also build credibility, uniqueness, and differentiation. For example, Tesla is a brilliant brand. In 2020, Tesla stock increased 700 percent in value. Elon Musk is such an amazing entrepreneur that NASA buys cargo and passenger space on his rockets. But what if Tesla decided to sell furniture, would you buy it? What if Johnson & Johnson consumer products decided to make electric cars? Would you assume the quality would be as good as Tesla? It's possible in the future, but not now.

This is the power of a brand. A respected brand convinces you to pay more. A brand can create confidence that the quality is good enough to buy. A brand you don't recognize will cause concern and even make you wary of a discount. How much would you pay for a Model S if Tesla's name wasn't on the car? In other words, it looks like a Model S and drives like a Model S, but it's made by an unknown manufacturer. Would you still pay $85,000? $50,000? $40,000? The unknown manufacturer says it is just as good as a Tesla. In other words, a well-known and respected car brand is worth tens of thousands of dollars in profit.

You can establish your own brand at a fraction of the cost that bigger companies pay. You can differentiate yourself from all other competitors. You can cause people to pay you more because of the credibility that your brand communicates. All this can be done with social media.

Social media help you build a brand by first targeting those who are likely to buy. It also helps you stay in communication in a way that would be too expensive if you advertised on mainstream media. It helps you engage in a way no other platform can provide.

First, figure out where your buyers are. Which platforms are they connected to? Which platforms do they spend the most time on? There are many other platforms besides Twitter, Facebook, and LinkedIn. Most of my potential prospects are on LinkedIn. Those who use it are likely sales pros or business owners trying to improve themselves and their organizations. Large corporate employees will also connect on LinkedIn, but may not spend as much time on the platform.

How to Build Your Brand

Post three times every week. Your posts should always include content benefiting the viewer. Posting messages about where you ate and pictures of your dog will be quickly ignored. The more often your posts are ignored, the less relevant you will be in the future. Think of those you have "Snoozed" or "Unfollowed" because their posts were a waste of time. But posting information about what you do and how it will benefit the viewer will be read and valued.

As I mentioned earlier, my son-in-law, Benji Hutchinson, a security executive, writes frequently on Facebook, Twitter, and LinkedIn about new capabilities of facial recognition. He posts about how it is used by the TSA at airports. He posts about airlines that do facial scans before they let you board international flights. He also posts that boarding passes are no longer needed when going through security. A facial scan is sufficient. It will access your whole itinerary. If you were connected to Benji on social media, you would probably read his posts because you are interested in how his information will impact you.

During one NBC news interview, the reporter confronted Benji about the lack of privacy facial recognition would create. Even though the interview was not altogether complimentary, Benji still posted it to every social media platform he was on. A wise advertising executive once said, "There is no negative PR. Any attention is good." Unless your picture is on a post office poster wanted by the FBI, you are building a brand.

Here are a few ways you can use social media to build your brand.

Try to connect with all your clients and prospects. As you talk to any prospect, search for them in social media. Send them a request to connect with a note that you enjoyed the meeting. Each time you talk to a client, do the same. Ask which platforms they are on and let them know you want to connect. They will expect an invitation. Do it the same day you interact. After more than one day, they may forget.

Connect with all of your webinar attendees. This seems like a lot of work. But you could give social media platform access to your assistant. They could search for webinar attendees and connect on your behalf. This can be effective if you post social media messages three times a week. Being top of mind is good advertising and will make your interpersonal sales more engaging.

Make video a weekly part of your social media posts. Video has and will continue to be the most engaging way to communicate. I pay a consultant to post my business-building tips three times a week on LinkedIn, Facebook, and Twitter. She also includes a short four-minute video of me at the end of the week. My videos get more engagement than any text.

Again, if messages are about your kids, a photo of a steak salad, or a beautiful sunset, you may lose attention. You are trying to build your brand, not advertising the local Italian restaurant. But if you make the message about something that will benefit the viewer, they will pay attention and remember you.

Many speakers like me post selfie videos from the stage of a presentation and discuss the event. This is usually recorded a few hours before or after the speech. It's kind of like, "This is what you missed by not being here" post. It's a really good idea since meeting planners may be looking for a speaker. It may be similar to what they are also planning.

I create videos advertising every speech, webinar, or virtual event I do. If I speak on referrals, I will film myself talking about how important referrals are and three things the audience gained as a result of attending. Before I speak at any event, I record a three-minute preview discussing why potential attendees should come and what they will gain from the presentation.

Source outside content that will benefit your prospects and clients. Content does not have to be unique to you. You can repost/share social media posts and blogs, including your favorite authors, information you read online, or even what your clients have gained as a result of working with you. It would be nice if you ask for permission first. But after forty years, it's amazing how many times my material is used without permission. The only rule is that it must benefit the viewer.

Always put a tagline of how you can be contacted. Put your website, email address, and your phone number on every post. Do not make viewers refer to your home page to get contact information. That causes friction. The easier you can make it for people to contact you, the more they will reach out. One way many of my coaching clients generate engagement is to offer a white paper, book, or videos as an incentive for viewers to follow up for more information.

One of my clients wrote a short book on retirement strategies. He posts on social media platforms three times a week and always includes his book offer. All the viewer has to do is call the telephone number and book an appointment. He usually puts a tagline in each post offering the book for free if they call and schedule a ten-minute phone call. It is very effective. He receives many calls every week.

How to Build Referrals Using Social Media
LINKEDIN

One of the reasons I like LinkedIn is that, once you connect with someone, you can look at all the people your new contact is connected to. When you connect to someone, you can see not only the 500 people in their network, but also search for more information about them like location, industry, experience, and even their hobbies.

It is easy to prospect for leads on LinkedIn. First, ask your clients if they are on that platform. Then ask if you can connect. They will always say yes. It will be tempting to procrastinate. But you need to connect within forty-eight hours. Your client will be looking for a notification to connect. Once you become a part of their network, you will be in a position to gain endless referrals.

Referrals are everything. As I wrote in my book *The Referral Mindset: 7 Easy Steps to EXPLOSIVE Growth from Your Own Customers*, referrals are 25 percent more likely to do business with you. They will spend 35 percent more with you than any other lead source. The real questions are: How do you get referrals? Is there a magic phrase? Why don't my clients just give me names because of my performance?

I write extensively in *The Referral Mindset* about having the right mindset for referrals and specifically what to say. But the best way to get referrals is not to ask. The best way to get referrals is to mine your clients' social media network.

Here's how to do it:

1. Ask your clients if you can connect on social media.
They will say yes. At that point look at all the people they are connected to. Spot anybody in their network that you would like to be introduced to? Click on their name and note any information such as hobbies, job title, and years of experience.

2. Talk to your A and B clients every three months.
A clients are your best and most profitable. They are defined as not only those you enjoy, but are also advocates. This means they refer business to you. B clients are defined as those you could make A clients out of if you kept in better contact.

The method of keeping in contact is to give A and B clients an update on any services that you provide or any information they would value. These could be relevant ideas from other clients. They could be related to economic data that might benefit them. Make the every-three-month phone call so informative the client always looks forward to talking.

3. Ask for referrals.

Stop using your old worn-out phrases like, "Don't keep me a secret," or "I get paid in two ways, the business we do and the referrals I get." These phrases are trite and inelegant. Instead use these sentences: "I really enjoy working with you. Most of your friends, family, and colleagues could use some of the things you are doing. Who do you know who could benefit from the kind of relationship we've had so far?"

Here is an example of how to ask for referrals from one of my financial advisor clients: "I really enjoy working with you. I'm not sure you know this but 83 percent of your friends and family will be totally dependent on social security sometime during their lives. Who do you know who could benefit from the kind of relationship we've had so far?"

Here is an example from one of my mortgage clients: "I really enjoy working with you. It's crazy that the average homeowner will refinance every three and a half years and purchase every seven years. They usually pay half a percent too much on each loan and don't have a broker who is looking out for them. Who do you know who could benefit from some of the things we have done?"

If you ask for referrals effectively, 38 percent of these requests will generate names. But even if you don't get a response, you are building advocacy. This is the mindset you can build in your client, motivating them to mention you. They will talk about you to their friends. Advocacy referrals have an 85 percent closing ratio. When people call you out of the blue because of a friend's suggestion, a sale is almost assured. That is the power of an advocacy referral.

4. Suggest four people you would like to meet from your client's social media network.

Don't forget. You have access to their social media network. You already picked out a few people you would like to be introduced to. You are simply asking to meet four people already in their network. Your client will know two of the four. Many wrongly use social media to build their self-worth. "The more people in my network, the more popular I am." This is not the kind of shallow network you want to build. Your goal should be to build relationships, not a blind virtual rolodex.

As you ask the client about people in their network, also ask who they know well. Is there something special about them? Do their kids play tennis? Did they just get back from vacation? You can use this information when you try to connect with the referral using social media.

5. Connect by mentioning your client.

As you contact the referral on social media, mention your client and possibly something unique about them. This is the personal info you discovered from the client. Any information like this will make you seem like a friend of a friend. It will help you connect and book appointments.

Recently, I sent a connection request to a contact from one of my clients. I knew he was a golfer. I asked in the invitation if he saw the Tiger Woods documentary on HBO. He responded immediately to my request and asked how often I played golf. I wish I had known earlier what a powerful magnet golf is. I might have been a pro golfer instead of a pro tennis player. A lot more people play golf.

6. After you connect, pick up the phone.

This is your chance to prospect for new business. Once the referred lead accepts your connection, ask to talk for ten minutes. Say you would like to find out more about them. You heard great things about them from your client. Suggest a specific time to talk. Perhaps they can talk at 10:40 a.m. on Thursday?

I've used this technique for nearly ten years. At least 65 percent of the people I connect to will agree to talk on the phone. One of the reasons this works so effectively is that it's so unique. Ninety-nine percent of the people who connect on any social media platform never communicate outside the platform. But you and I both know that a relationship is built with an interpersonal connection, not on social media threads. It would be ideal if you could meet for a cup of coffee. But short of that, a virtual video or audio call is good enough.

7. Use the Five-Step Bridge.

Here's a step-by-step process of what to do on the call.

Introduce yourself, mention the referral source, and engage: "John, my name is Kerry Johnson. We have a mutual friend named Dan Thompson. You remember Dan, don't you?"

Elevator speech. Let them know who you are. Don't pitch: "Did Dan say anything about me? Can I give you some background? I'm a financial advisor with Johnson Financial."

Offer your three unique bullet points: "I do three things for my clients. I make sure their retirement lasts as long as they do. I take all the volatility out of their investments, and I decrease taxes when they are ready to take money out of their retirement."

Tell a story: "A few years ago, I was introduced to a seventy-year-old woman named Sally. She was retired for only five years and terrified. Sally lost 35 percent of her portfolio because of risky assets that lost money. She said, 'Please don't make me go back to work as a greeter at Walmart!' I took a look at the portfolio and noticed that she was indeed in the kinds of investments that would work for a twenty-five-year-old. But not at seventy. We rebalanced and took a lot of the risk out. During the last downturn, she didn't lose a penny. She came to my office last week and brought my favorite Starbucks chai tea latte with a bundt cake she made herself. We laughed that she wasn't yet working at Walmart. When I get clients like that, it makes me feel like everything I do is worth it."

Segue to the prospect: "I'm not sure if all this will benefit you. But I would love to find out more about you first."

Did you notice the steps used in the good elevator speech? First, you need to label yourself and then engage. Next, state three benefits you do better than all other competitors. Then tell a story. Last, segue to your referred-lead prospect.

Use the Five-Step Bridge

I discussed earlier how to use the Five-Step Bridge. You can refer to the section on how to book appointments and webinars using this process. The Five-Step Bridge is the Swiss Army knife of sales success. It prevents you from pitching. It allows you to sell without selling. Close without closing. It allows you to listen and find out what the prospect's needs and concerns are. Once you learn those, an appointment is generated nearly every time.

Here are the steps using the Five-Step Bridge with social media contacts:

YOU: "Thanks for listening to my elevator speech. Tell me more about yourself."

SOCIAL MEDIA LEAD: "I am a retired exec with IBM. I have a few grandkids and travel a little also."

YOU: "Great. Our buddy John was concerned about taxes going up with the new US president. Does that concern you?"

SOCIAL MEDIA LEAD: "Yes. I think any retiree has to think about taxes. I get social security and a distribution from my IRA."

YOU: "What are you doing right now to mitigate taxes from your IRA?"

SOCIAL MEDIA LEAD: "No plan really."

YOU: "How about social security taxes? Depending on where you live, that can also be taxed."

SOCIAL MEDIA LEAD: "We are thinking about moving to Florida so I don't think they tax social security. But the IRS is different."

You: "What about family? Is leaving a legacy important to you?"

Social Media Lead: "Yes, I put myself through grad school and struggled the whole time financially. I would love to create a tuition fund for my grandkids."

You: "If I heard you correctly, you want to mitigate IRA taxes, but don't have a plan. You also believe taxes will increase, but other than moving to Florida, you don't have a plan to lower those taxes either. You also would like to create a tuition fund for your grandkids. Did I get all that right?"

Social Media Lead: "Absolutely."

You: "If we could talk more about how to decrease IRA taxes, avoid social security tax increases, and plan for your grandkids, would that be helpful?"

Social Media Lead: "Yes. What do you have in mind?"

FACEBOOK

While it is easy to connect on Facebook, it is much more difficult to see the connections. You undoubtedly are a member of Facebook groups. When you join, you gain the opportunity to click on group member profiles as another way to engage. Then "Friend" members you are interested in. Once they accept your connection, you can ask to speak by video or audio for ten minutes using the skills I discussed with LinkedIn.

Use Groups to Prospect

One of the best ways to lead-generate on Facebook is by using groups. Joining a group is easy. I am a member of at least ten groups. Three are Americans in Portugal. Two are American Airlines–related, since I am a top-level Executive Platinum flyer. And three others are cancer-related since I am a cancer survivor.

The membership of my groups ranges anywhere from 800 to 12,000. To be honest, any group with more than 5,000 will be unwieldy since there are so many posts. But if you can stay active, you will build awareness and possibly a brand. From there you just have to be open to new opportunities. Here are some steps to use in gaining leads from groups:

Search for likely groups.
Do a Facebook search and find your target groups. There are groups for every conceivable topic ranging from retirees to Range Rover enthusiasts.

When you are accepted into a group, introduce yourself with an initial post.
Some admins frown on this, but only because it takes too much time. They just don't want to clog their pages with bios from every new member. Most new entrants never post. But if you want to build brand awareness, an intro is critical.

Private Message (PM) when you see opportunities.
Read posts from your groups often. Questions are asked every-where. If you see an opportunity to help or answer a question, send a PM to the member. Usually, admins don't want outright sales pitches. But few will push back on private messages between two members. Their goal is to keep and build their membership—not to stop you from making money.

Call and use the Five-Step Bridge.

Once you private message a member, offer to talk on the phone. Let them know you can be more helpful if you can talk for a few minutes. Since you have the Five-Step Bridge tool, you will never pitch or sell. You will only find needs and offer solutions.

Using groups will generate at least one opportunity per day per group. You could build your business using Facebook alone. It is that effective. But you are a pro and have many lead-generation methods to choose from.

Talking to your Facebook contacts is a risk. If you decide to pitch or sell, it may get back to the group that you are inappropriately marketing yourself. But by using the Five-Step Bridge and listening, you will always be elegant and never get pushback. You will simply listen for opportunities and suggest solutions as you discover needs.

TWITTER

This platform has the least opportunity for engagement of the major social media platforms. You can follow somebody and respond to posts. Even though it is much more difficult to connect individually, you can still engage with others based on their responses and profile.

You can't look at your Twitter connections' networks. But you can look at the people who respond to posts. When you find somebody interesting, engage them and ask to find out more. Request a virtual video or audio call and, again, use the Five-Step Bridge. The only reason anybody would deny your request to talk is if they felt you were going to pitch them. But if you mention that you want to find out more, most people will be interested in a short ten-minute call. One of the reasons this works is because nobody else does it. Think of the last time someone asked to talk to you based on a social media connection.

Not once in all my years on social media has anybody asked to connect via video or phone. Not once. If someone did ask to talk, I first would want to know if they had an agenda. Were they going to try to sell me something? I get about five requests per day to connect. They are usually selling lead-generation services, PR, or some other service promising to double my business. I usually dismiss those requests. But if I do connect, I always first ask to talk on the phone.

Recently, I responded to a request to connect on LinkedIn from someone who promised to increase my sales. I sent a message back that I was suspicious of their pitch since they knew nothing about me. I got a boilerplate response saying how wonderful they are and why I should use them. This pathetic note is the best you will get. Your competition in getting business from social media is nonexistent. Nobody is willing to talk. If you connect and ask to talk to find out more, you will be successful. As long as you don't pitch or sell. If a connection is first interested in finding out more about me, I would be glad to talk. As long as I feel I'm not exposing myself to a sales pitch, I would be glad to spend ten minutes on the phone. You will find similar success with the people you engage with on social media.

Think of the advocacy you will gain if you use these steps. You can spend $200 buying a lead. Or $300 attracting a prospect to a webinar. You can even give up 50 percent of your commissions by accepting appointments scheduled by companies that advertise services on TV. For example, when you see an air conditioning advertisement with a phone number, you will get at least ten sales calls. The lead providers often split sales with the caller.

Mainstream advertising is expensive. You can spend $25,000 on a TV or radio ad, hoping for some kind of response. It's hard to just break even. Or you can use the techniques I discussed to engage with social media contacts. If you are smart, you will use the Five-Step Bridge during the call. Your closing ratio will be enormously high without the cost of advertising. All you have to do is utilize your social media connections.

Magazine Articles

Part of building a brand in the online world is being recognized. Often that means being known as an expert. Those who build sales, either virtually or in person, build brands using not only tools like a succinct elevator speech, but also an effective website. They also communicate their expertise and brand by frequently writing for the magazines and newsletters their prospects and clients read.

Have you ever asked clients what mass communication they pay attention to? Do they read a community newspaper? Do they read a national magazine? What blogs do they like? In my little town of Tustin, California, we have a little community newspaper called *The Sentry*. It is really only about ten pages and publishes weekly. At least five pages are full of small boxed, cheap advertising. There is both an online and physical version.

There is also room for commentary from experts like you who could add value. For example, a real estate agent could write an article about how to best buy a property. A mortgage broker could write about where interest rates are headed and the changing terms of federally backed mortgages. A financial advisor could write about how to create wealth, or at least how not to lose it. You know the topics you could write on.

I write for at least ten magazines a month. My promise to publishers is that I will never submit an article to their competition. It is surprisingly easy to get your articles published. Just call the editor or publisher and ask if they would consider your submissions. It's important that you be prepared with an elevator speech and how your expertise would benefit their readers. Most magazine articles allow for about 800 words, or two pages. You should always include your picture and a bio at the end and how you can be contacted.

The real benefit of writing is not just direct advertising. It is the PR benefit of sending a new prospect a few articles from a magazine they recognize. It builds credibility, competence in your ability, and a belief in your brand. Think of the brand differentiation you could command at a party. Someone might ask what you do. You could deliver an elevator speech and mention that you write for a magazine they recognize. Would you have more impact on them than all the other people they know in your industry?

When someone asks what I do for living, I typically say I'm the best-selling author of sixteen books and speak at conventions around the world. I write for ten magazines every month. If I know what the prospect does, I will mention a magazine that most closely matches their industry. Invariably, they will say, "Oh, I must've read you before someplace." Think of the credibility you would have meeting a prospect and letting them know that you write for a publication they read.

Magazines are not the only vehicles you could write for. Others could be industry newsletters, local publications, or even a blog that targets your market. But don't expect these editors to call you because you are good. You still have to market yourself. You still have to make contact and use the Five-Step Bridge to find out what editors need. Then make an offer to write. Don't expect or ask for payment. The exposure is enough.

Social media are not the only platforms people pay attention to. They still read online magazines, hardcover publications, and industry newsletters. The more you write for these, the more effectively you can build your brand. When you have a recognizable brand, sales come easier. Your closing ratio will increase. You will make more money.

Newsletters

An overlooked, yet effective way to advertise is using your own targeted newsletters. The focus, of course, can be your clients and prospects. For some reason, many salespeople believe that once a sale is transacted, the relationship ends. The reality is that your clients, according to Forrester Research, want three things:

1. To understand the functionally of what they are buying.
2. To be confident that you are in control, that you will always do what is best for them.

3. To have frequent relationship communication. They want to keep in virtual or face-to-face contact with you every few months, even after the sale is completed.

I often encounter coaching candidates with hundreds of clients. I always ask how often they keep in contact with their As and Bs. Clients are customers you have a relationship with. A customer is only a transaction. Most send Christmas and birthday cards. Some brag about an email newsletter sent a few times a year. Shooting a timely text or email is always a good idea. If you have the discipline to send a monthly email update, you will be able to at least be remembered more than if you never spoke to the customer again. But if you want to create clients from customers, you need to build a post-sale relationship.

But very few vendors and salespeople keep in contact via phone, video, or face-to-face. We know that people buy relationships first, products and services second. We also know the stronger the relationship, the more likely you are to get referrals. So, doesn't it make sense to keep in contact with your clients every three months no matter what the platform?

Newsletters are only good for branding. They do not produce sales. They can be marketing vehicles in helping you build a virtual relationship. Like branding, marketing does not build sales. Interpersonal relationships do. When you produce frequent newsletters or post on social media, you are only building a stage to support a better personal relationship. The relationship is what matters. A fact-filled newsletter will help build your brand and streamline your virtual calls.

I recommend that you email or snail mail a monthly newsletter to every client and prospect. It is easy to see why newsletters are important to keep in contact with clients. It seems less important to send them to prospects.

Prospects don't buy for many reasons. The timing may not have been right. There may have been a lower price from a competitor. Possibly they were not ready, but could be now. It's all about timing. You just need to be there when the time is right. That's why it's so critical to send prospects a newsletter every month instead of quarterly.

Just because somebody said no today does not mean no forever. All you have to do is keep in contact. While I hate to lose a coaching client, there is a 65 percent chance they will reengage me within five years. All I have to do is keep in contact.

How to Keep in Contact

Send a one-page newsletter every month. It can be email or a hard snail-mail copy. The newsletter must be relevant with information the prospect and client can use. It could be the five concerns that retirees have. It could be the three reasons to consider buying an investment property. It could be how to increase your FICO score. It doesn't matter the topic. What matters is whether the reader can use the information.

I get a monthly newsletter from a local real estate agent. What I value most is the update on the average listing price per square foot and the average sales price for homes in my area. It also displays trend lines comparing home prices from last year to today.

There are always tidbits on what buyers care most about. The agent often posts information on how much a seller spent on a kitchen or bathroom. Is it worth it to replaster a pool? These are all areas that readers value and will remember.

Sending a newsletter is unlikely to produce sales. But it does build a brand. Newsletters, mailings, and advertising may generate incoming phone calls, but don't depend on it. The answer is the Three-Month Phone Call. Every client or prospect should have your cell phone number. Make sure you ask them to put you on their contact list. That way, you will be identified when your cell number comes up on their phone. It doesn't matter the demographic; the three-month call works. You just have to be patient and be prepared to leave four voicemails for every one you connect with.

Because of Forrester Research, we know clients want frequent contact with you. But prospects do too. The reason most salespeople don't call prospects is because they don't know what to say. There are only so many times you can ask a prospect if they are ready to buy. If that's all you have to say, the prospect won't answer the phone. It's the same with a client. If all you asked was whether they had any questions, the client would let the call go to voicemail every time.

There are many versions of the virtual sale. One is obvious. The video platform. But the other is a phone. Anything that isn't a face-to-face contact should be thought of as virtual. But anytime you can do a video instead of an audio call will develop more rapport. When you gain more rapport, you also gain more trust.

The three-month call should be scheduled as a video platform call. For example, before you end your current client or prospect call, suggest a follow-up call in three months. Then ask if they would mind doing it via video. If they agree, great. If they would rather talk on their cell, that is fine also. But always make the video platform the preferable mode of contact.

The Three-Month Phone Call

Here is a three-part process that will build your business by a minimum of 38 percent in thirty days. It will work whether you call using video or only audio. The steps are the same.

1. CATCH UP

Calling a prospect or client every three months requires a workable customer relationship manager platform or CRM. Hopefully you wrote down the last conversation in your notes. Perhaps the client has a new grandchild. Maybe the prospect just returned from a Mediterranean cruise. Possibly they were in the process of selling their house when you last spoke. Whatever it was, start your call by referencing your last conversation.

2. UPDATE

This is why your prospect or client will answer the phone. They look forward to hearing information they can use. But it's important that you discuss ideas that are relevant and helpful. It could be current home values or where interest rates are headed. You could even talk about what you see happening in the stock market over the next three months. Anything to get the conversation started.

The rule of thumb is to do no more than a three-minute update. Any more is counterproductive. The purpose of the update is to get your prospect or client to engage. It is not to impress them with how much you know.

3. THE FIVE-STEP BRIDGE AND REFERRAL

This is the place to find out needs and book appointments. I discussed this earlier in the section on confirming appointments, but here is how to use this technique in the Three-Month Phone Call setting.

Introductory sentence.

Ask what their thoughts are about your updates. For example, ask how market volatility may affect them. Ask how increasing interest rates might influence their decision to buy property this year. If you are a mortgage broker, you might ask about any credit card debt they might have. Will rising interest rates increase their credit card payments?

Search for needs (get three).

This is the time to listen. You need to set the stage to book appointments. As you ask about their stock market exposure, you also want to know whether their portfolio has too much volatility. As a real estate agent, you might ask about their next move or plans on purchasing investment property. It's all in how you probe. Never pitch. Nobody wants to be sold. But they are very interested in buying. It's always a question about what their goals are and what they want.

Gaining needs.

Timing. Just because a prospect said no now doesn't mean forever. You need to contact prospects every three months because a no now might be yes in a few months. If they selected another vendor because of a discount today, there could be future disappointment when their expectations are not met. If you call them every three months, there is a 38 percent chance they will be ready to buy because you called at the right time.

Call Prospects Every Three Months

Clients are current relationships with those you are doing business with. Prospects are those you have spoken to who have not yet done business with you. Unlike a client, the prospect call is different. Any time you speak to a prospect or client, get three needs and put them in your notes. You can use these needs during your next call. Here's how the conversation might go:

"The last time we spoke, you were very concerned about taxes, volatility, and ensuring that your retirement money lasts as long as you do. What have you done so far to find answers to those concerns?"

They likely haven't done anything. At that point, ask if the needs are still important to them. If so, recap and trial-close as I have discussed earlier. Even if they have purchased from another vendor, they may be currently disappointed. You need to be persistent.

Hurt and Rescue: How to Find Needs When There Aren't Any

Have you ever spoken to a prospect or client who didn't seem to need what you sell? Have you ever been challenged in getting them to talk? You need skill when you search for needs. Often it entails presenting a problem and asking the prospect or client how they would handle it.

If you are a financial advisor, for example, and see stock market volatility in the future, you might ask the client how they would prevent a loss. If you are a mortgage broker and see rising interest rates in the future, you might ask a prospect with an adjustable loan how they would prevent a $200 monthly payment increase. If you were selling real estate investment services to flippers, you might ask how they would deal with a loss of carrying a property too long. What would they do?

Hurt and rescue is one of the most effective ways of producing needs. It is useful in getting a prospect to think about the future and eventually ask for your solutions. If the prospect says they don't care about an issue, you can simply move on to another concern. Or even offer to call them in another three months to check up. They will always answer the phone if you present information they can use.

Here's an example of how you would use hurt and rescue in discovering needs. I assume that you have done the catch-up and update part of the Three-Month Phone Call. You could even use hurt and rescue to upsell.

"One of my concerns is what would happen if you contracted a long-term illness. The assisted care facility can cost up to $12,000 per month or more. Most medical insurance will not pay for a long-term stay. How would you pay for that? Does that concern you?"

They will either ask for your recommendation, or deflect, saying they really don't care. If they deflect, just move on. If they ask for your help, recap, trial-close, and book a follow-up appointment (explained next). In a client call, you could provide a solution on the spot. After all, they have already bought from you and trust your recommendations. But never present a solution during a prospect call. You don't want them taking your solution to a competitor. You need to schedule a virtual audio or video call or face-to-face follow-up. Then use the 333 presentation process, explained earlier, as you present.

The next part of the Three-Month Phone Call is to **recap** the three needs you heard on the call. I have discussed how to do this earlier, but it's always good to use their own words as you recap.

For example: "If I heard correctly, you are concerned about how you would pay for a long-term illness, what you would do if we had another stock market shock like 2020, and whether your retirement assets will last as long as you do. Did I get that right?"

The recap is the psychotherapeutic model of selling. It forces you to listen. It makes people feel understood. This is such an important concept that if you apply it effectively, your closing ratio will double. Don't limit the recap to only those calls that may result in a sale. Use the recap on every communication that you engage in. Practice it. Make it part of your communication style. Make it a mindset. If you do, your prospects will feel understood and your closing ratio will increase dramatically.

An example of the **trial close** is this: "If we could take a look at how to pay for a long-term illness, prevent a shock like we had in 2020, and make sure that your retirement assets last as long as you do, with that be helpful?"

The trial close is your chance to gain commitment. If you trial-close their three needs, and you present relevant solutions to only those three needs, your closing ratio will always be 85 to 100 percent.

If you can **book an appointment** after the trial close, wait to ask for a **referral**. But if you cannot find needs and aren't able to book an appointment, ask for a referral on the spot. As I discussed earlier, referrals are 25 percent more likely to do business with you and will produce 35 percent more income. The problem is not that you are asking the wrong way; the issue is that you aren't asking at all. You could ask clients to connect on LinkedIn. That way you could use LinkedIn referral techniques and look at all the people they are connected to. You could then choose the prospects you would like to be introduced to.

The Three-Month Phone Call is the perfect way to get a referral on the spot. In fact, 38 percent of the Three-Month Phone Calls will produce at least one referral.

Let me discuss two kinds of referrals:

Proactive referrals. This is your chance to get a name. For more information on what to say to referred leads, read my book *The Referral Mindset: 7 Easy Steps to EXPLOSIVE Growth.*

Advocacy referrals. These are the kinds of referrals that call you out of the blue. For example, a client may call and mention a friend who will be expecting your phone call. Another version of an advocacy referral is when the friend calls you directly and mentions your client. The referral will probably discuss concerns and ask for your help.

The difference between proactive and advocacy referrals is closing ratios. A proactive referral has a 38 percent chance of generating a name you can call later. An advocacy referral has an 85 percent chance of booking a sale right now. An advocacy referred lead will call you with a concern. This lead has already bought you emotionally because of the strength of the current client's endorsement.

Many years ago, my client Tom received a phone call from an advocacy referral resulting in a booked appointment. The prospect walked in Tom's office and started talking about his needs and concerns. Tom discussed his services. Ten minutes into the meeting, the prospect took out a checkbook and wrote a retainer for $1 million. He asked Tom who it should be payable to.

Tom said, "Our first consult is free. I just wanted to get to know you better and find out how I can help."

The advocacy referral said, "I was ready to buy before I walked in the office. I just wanted to make sure that you could fog a mirror." That's the power of advocacy referrals.

The only way to get advocacy referrals, the holy grail of sales, is frequency of contact. The more you contact your clients, the more referrals you will get from them. Referrals are never based on your competence and brilliance. If that were the case, the smartest sales pros would always get the most business. That is simply not true. Relationships are the building blocks of advocacy referrals. If you keep in contact with your A and B clients every three months, your business will increase by a minimum of 38 percent. Most of my clients who use this technique are able to double their business the first year and increase sales by 38 percent every year after.

I learned a lesson twenty years ago in the Minneapolis airport on my way to a speech. Before I left on the trip, I had bought a new handheld database gadget called the Pilot Pen. It was a rudimentary electronic rolodex including only name, contact information, and a few notes. When I landed in Minneapolis, I accidentally clicked on a speaking client who lived nearby. I used a pay phone (that's how long ago it was) and called him to catch up. We chatted for a few minutes while I updated him on some new seminar ideas he said were useful. He was really enthusiastic about the call. After a few minutes of talking, he remarked that his company was planning a leaders' retreat in a few months and asked if I would consider being the keynote speaker.

He didn't really care about my speaking fee. He didn't even seem interested in considering other speakers. It was just me. I am totally convinced that I called at the right time. I kept in contact every three months after the event and received many more referrals. If you really want to build your business, you will keep in contact with every A and B client and qualified prospects every three months.

7

The Wedge:
How to Erase the Competition

Have you ever contacted a lead who already had a vendor? Perhaps you are a mortgage broker and want to gain more real estate agents to refer business. They are currently giving business to your competition. You could be a real estate agent cold calling for listings. You reach a homeowner who replies that their next move will be with their last agent. You may be a financial advisor who hears that an investor is happy with their current broker. Do you just walk away? What should you do?

Many of the skills you could use in a face-to-face environment need to be even more elegant on a virtual platform. The virtual sale is more abbreviated and succinct. Your sales skills must be even more honed for the virtual contact.

Follow these three solid rules in erasing the competition.

1. **Most clients don't want to be sold, but they are willing to buy.** I have discussed at length the importance of listening. When you pitch or sell, people feel talked at or sold to.

2. **People feel the best ideas are the ones they think of themselves.** You are likely not persuasive enough to convince people to buy from you. They have to think of reasons to buy on their own. It has to be their idea. You can only set the stage for them to decide.

3. **There are three people in every sale: You, the prospect, and their current vendor.** One of the reasons your closing ratio is low is that you believe you are selling to only one prospect. Whether the spouse is present, a friend, or even a corporate complex sale, it is always you, the prospect, and the current vendor. It is always a triangle that some call the incumbent vendor.

Even though you have a better idea, a way to save money, or even a way to solve a problem, the prospect must always be willing to change from what they are currently doing. They have to first sever the relationship. Most people have a dependency on the status quo. They likely will avoid change because staying the same is always easier. Ask about competitors as you probe. Listen emotionally for clues as to whether they are working with other vendors. Even if the prospect doesn't mention any competition, they may bring it up later.

Many years ago, I contacted an executive with a major company. He was referred by one of my clients. I chatted for a few minutes and went through the Five-Step Bridge. It was actually too easy. I was suspicious. He loved our conversation and looked forward to talking later. I also knew his upcoming event was about three months away. Usually, I am booked to speak anywhere from six months to two years from a convention date. I asked if he had any speakers lined up. He did but hadn't sent any contracts out yet. But he had planned to that week. I immediately applied The Wedge and booked the event. I explain shortly.

Getting through the Stall

Stalling often means the prospect will tell you what you want to hear and then call their current vendor. The displaced vendor will do everything they can to conserve business. The most powerful weapon in their arsenal is to create doubt. This will cause your potential client to avoid confusion and do nothing.

When you are face-to-face, you can read emotions more effectively. You also have a greater chance of generating rapport. But in a virtual environment, it is easier to stall. After all, all the prospect has to do is tell you they want to think about it and hang up. When you are in front of a person, the prospect is likely to offer a more detailed explanation of their reasoning and communicate more candidly. Because there is often less rapport on the virtual call, stalls can occur more frequently.

One financial advisor presented a retirement plan. The prospect was excited and said things like, "I can't wait to get this started, I wish I had done this ten years ago," and "I look forward to moving my accounts to you."

But then the committed prospect took everything she heard right back to the old advisor. The incumbent advisor immediately created doubt. The incumbent advisor said to watch out for the hidden fees, the risk is much greater than he would've recommended, and there is a likelihood that she is wasting money. The client became nervous.

The advisor said, "The hidden fees are $10,000 more than our plan now. How much risk are you willing to take? You will lose everything if you move your money."

The prospect then responded, "Do you really think I could lose money with this?" All the incumbent advisor had to do was create doubt. The prospect was scared and, because of status quo bias, chose to do nothing.

The answer is this:

- The prospect needs to fire the incumbent vendor before you present a solution.
- You first have to get out of the way. Allow the prospect to tell you what they don't like about their current vendor.
- You have to listen to the prospect talk about their advisor relationship before you can sell a new one.

The Incumbent Vendor Relationship

Before the prospect will make a change, they may get one last opinion from the current vendor. This will allow the incumbent to match your solution and often improve it. Since the standing relationship is much stronger than the new one with you, the old vendor is likely to win. All they have to do is present a product or service like yours. And because of the established relationship, they win. Your response often is to push harder with logic. But since the existing relationship is based on rapport and trust, you will lose. You can argue details and features. The client probably only understands the product functionally. They don't really care about the details that you think are so important.

You may say something like, "We can save 3 percent on commissions by doing this. You will never take a loss again with this approach. Over the last ten years, we would have increased your returns by 35 percent."

These are all logical arguments. But the incumbent vendor can match those benefits, especially if they face losing existing business. The client may think, "The devil I know is better than the one I don't."

NEVER ATTACK THE INCUMBENT

If you ever attack an incumbent vendor or their current service, the prospects may feel compelled to defend themselves. This makes a lot of sense. "If you point out my mistakes, I will justify and rationalize. I may even resent you." This will also cause the prospect to block you in the future. Recently a colleague told me his way to originate new business was a radio show. I told him radio was expensive, and time-consuming, as well as not productive in building business. I wanted to point out his mistake. Instead, he defended the strategy and the conversation ended.

Recently, I had internet connection problems in my office. My usual IT guy was unavailable. I called another networking expert to take a look. He spent the first hour trashing my network installed by the IT guy I had used for ten years. I made excuses for my tech and never used the new IT guy again.

THE INSTANT REPLAY TECHNIQUE

People don't change. Who you were ten years ago is substantially the way you are today. Except for a new hairstyle, car, and a better golf swing, you are still you. In fact, the revered child development psychologist Piaget said that certain levels of personality are laid in concrete by the age of seven. Sure, you can learn. You can adapt, develop, and improve. But the core of who you are is still that kid at seven years old.

If you believe this notion that people don't change, does it also make sense that we don't change buying behavior either? The way to apply this is called instant Replay. We need to get prospects to tell us how they made their last buying decision.

Here is an example of what you could say: "Who did you use to list your house last time? How did you decide to work with that last agent? What about them made you decide they were right for you?"

This type of questioning could be confusing. Most prospects have never been asked this. They may move into System 1 (introduced earlier) and tell you how they met the agent instead of how they decided to hire them. Here is what you should say: "I understand that you both play tennis at the same club. But why them? Why not another real estate agent? Selling your house is a big deal. What was it about them that made you say yes?"

At this point the prospect will drill down: "I guess it was the fact that they knew my neighborhood. They knew how much my home should be listed for. They also offered to stage the furniture. That was a big deal since ours wasn't that nice."

Guess how that homeowner will decide on the next person to sell their home? It will be local knowledge of the market and staging the house.

THE LET'S ASSUME TECHNIQUE

This is absolutely the most powerful probing question you can ever ask. Asking the let's assume question will actually give the prospect a chance to tell you what they want to buy. All you have to do is listen and sell it to them.

Here is the question: "Let's assume it's ten years in the future. What happened that let you know you the retirement plan was perfect and we had a great relationship?"

Here are three steps to follow:

1. **Don't interrupt.** You need three answers. If you talk, they will get distracted and you won't find out what they want to buy.

2. **Drill their emotions down to numbers.** Being happy is an emotion. Being happy because you are getting $5,000 a month in retirement is a number.

3. **Use the trial close.** Commit to what they want to buy. Just like using the Five-Step Bridge, trial-close their three needs and ask if they would like to hear about how to find solutions to those needs on the next appointment.

Here is an example of how I used the let's assume technique in booking a speech.

> ME: "Ms. Meeting Planner (MP), let's assume the event is over. What did the group get from the presentation that was most valued?"
>
> MP: "I guess it was a good speech."
>
> ME: "But what specifically did they get that made the most difference?"
>
> MP: "I suppose the group walked away with better ways to close more business. I also hope they learned how to manage their time better. And I hope they left with more motivation to hit their goals."
>
> ME: "So, if I have this straight, if we could focus on closing techniques, time management, and motivation to hit their goals right now, would that be helpful?"
>
> MP: "Great. What do you have in mind?"

I could have presented one of my standard speeches. I also could have risked rejection. But all I had to do was present what she wanted. Everything else was easy.

ASK ABOUT PERFECTION

Let's assume for the moment that your prospect isn't very candid and won't discuss their current vendor. The best technique here is to ask about perfection. Tell them what perfection is and whether they are getting it.

Here is an example from the mortgage industry: "I know you have a mortgage broker right now. But I'd like to ask a question. A perfect mortgage relationship is helping you erase any bad credit reporting, talking every couple of days about the loan progress, paying for all closing costs, and always getting at least a quarter point discount off the best rates available. I'm curious, are these important to you? Did you get these on your last loan?"

When they say no, which they usually will, ask which they didn't get. Also ask which are the most important. Then trial-close and present solutions.

Here is an example from the financial services industry:

REP: "Our goal is to prevent our clients from losing any money. Research from Jeremy Siegel at the Wharton Business School has shown that for every 20 percent loss, you must get a return of 40 percent just to break even. Tell me about your investment returns over the last ten years. Did you take any losses?"

PROSPECT: "Well yeah, I did. But didn't everybody?"

REP: "Actually, not one of our clients lost a penny. I'm sure that was also the case with you, right?"

PROSPECT: "I wasn't so lucky. I lost 35 percent over the last two years in the last downturn."

REP: "So, under Siegel, it now will take you a 70 percent return to get back to even. Are you okay with that?"

PROSPECT: "No. I'm very irritated. I can't believe that I made such big mistakes."

REP: "Well, it's not your fault. Yet I am sure your advisor probably worked hard to get the best returns they could. I'm sure the advisor called you at least every three months and probably also diversified your account so that one asset class increased while the other decreased, mitigating your losses, right?"

PROSPECT: "No. I wish he had done that."

REP: "What would you like me to do?"

PROSPECT: "I just don't want to lose any more money."

REP: "If we could make sure you don't lose another penny, keep in close contact, and always keep you in the loop, would that be a better way to go?"

Through this questioning process, you are not attacking their strategy or relationship. You are not creating blame for their financial mistakes, and definitely not pitching. But through this probing process, you are able to create a wedge between them and their advisor. Only then can you present solutions they will accept.

AVOID BEING THE SAME

It's critical that you differentiate yourself from their incumbent vendor. If you are the same as they currently have, status quo wins. But if you can listen first to what they want, and then how you are better specifically in those areas, you will create differentiation. If you try to match strengths, you lose. But if you find out the incumbent's weaknesses, and present your strengths in those areas, you will create a wedge.

If you wanted to buy a car and every dealership had the exact color and style, you'd always go for the lowest price. Yet that is often what you do in competing with other vendors. You present exactly what people have heard before and expect them to do business with you. Or you present what their current vendor also suggests. Again, status quo wins.

LATENT WEDGE

It has often been said that you need to find the pain in order to administer a cure. But pain may be latent. It may have been there all along. You just have to get the prospect to talk about it. All I really have to do is present a perfect scenario and challenge the prospect to be honest. That creates a need I could sell to.

One way to apply the latent wedge is to ask what they dislike about working with vendors in general. My frustration in working with mortgage brokers is they accept or deny loans and never let me know why. Real estate agents seem to make homeowners into monetary transactions by never following up after the sale. My CPA has never checked in outside of tax time. Even after buying high-end Porsches, I have never had a dealer call to follow up. For me, these are all examples of the latent wedge. The way you apply this is to simply ask what bothers the prospect most about those in your industry. Or what they would generally like to improve. Your prospects will rarely be shy about sharing.

Preserving the Separation

Once you've created a wedge between the prospect and the former advisor, you then have to prepare the prospect for the incumbent vendor call. You have just replaced their business. They lost a sale. You can bet they will call the client.

One way to do this is as follows:

REP: I'm glad that we have found some areas we can help. But there's one more step. Your vendor is going to lose a lot of money in commissions and fees. They are likely to try as hard as they can to keep your business. They will tell you the company can offer the same service with the same products. But yet they haven't done it in all the years you have been with them. What will you say?"

PROSPECT: "It depends on what he says."

REP: "I can tell you what he is going to say. He will offer the same things you and I spoke about, and try to improve the relationship. *But when somebody shows you who they are, you should believe them.* The improvements will last a short time but will revert to what you were getting before. How are you going to respond when he says that?"

PROSPECT: "I'm not going to stand for more of the same. I won't let him do that."

REP: "Let me tell you a story of one my clients who also had a vendor like yours [story here]. Do you know what to say to him now?"

PROSPECT: "I know exactly what to do."

If you can coach your prospect on the responses the incumbent advisor is likely to give, and prepare them for what the advisor will say to conserve the relationship, you will insert a wedge between the prospect and their vendor.

Conclusion

The virtual sale is all about creating engagement, using both video and audio. It is critical to have sound, fast internet, and make sure the video is framed and set up to avoid distractions. Generating rapport and trust during any call is the most important part. In the end, a virtual sale is like any other. Selling is all about relationships. It is all about listening and making people feel understood and is never about pitching or thinking your products and services will sell themselves.

Sales is about finding needs and producing solutions. It is about prospecting by keeping in contact every three months. A lot of folks think we will go back to the office and hold face-to-face meetings soon. We went through a system shock with the COVID-19 pandemic. We'll have more shocks. Remote work and virtual communication are here to stay. The mix of virtual and in-person forms of contact will always be with us. This book teaches you how to use both in your prospecting and client communication.

COVID-19 taught us we can do business anywhere. We can talk to prospects in our living room. We can lead a fifty-person webinar from a home office. We can attend a virtual convention without ever setting foot in a hotel ballroom. But we can't take the relationship out of any sale. As we reengage in more face-to-face meetings, we will still use the same skill sets that built sales before the pandemic.

Like it or not, COVID-19 taught us that we won't always be able to meet face-to-face. It also taught us how important relationships are no matter what the environment. We can't replace relationships and trust. If it were not for your interpersonal skills, your company would bypass you in a heartbeat as a redundant cost. They would simply sell from a website. It's all about your ability to generate leads and maintain relationships that adds the greatest value.

If anything, the virtual sales environment showed us how valuable people skills really are to the process. We can't just order online. We can't build a business without making interpersonal contact. But we can automate the beginning of the process. We can use more text messaging, email marketing, social media engagement, and even more branding by writing articles.

Once we gain a qualified lead, we need to engage them personally as we go through the sales process. We need to listen for needs, recap like a therapist, and keep in frequent contact. We can automate the process to schedule those engagements. We can calendar calls more effectively. We can remind prospects to decrease no-shows. We can send short video demo introductions. But the process is still about the people. It is still about your ability to connect, listen, and present relevant solutions that will build your business in any environment. The virtual sale is just a more sophisticated platform to do it in.

Please contact me at
kerry@kerryjohnson.com
Twitter: @DrKerryJohnson
LinkedIn: Kerry Johnson, MBA, PhD
Phone: (714) 368-3650

Send me a note. I would love to hear about your results.

www.ingramcontent.com/pod-product-compliance
Lightning Source LLC
Jackson TN
JSHW011934131224
75386JS00041B/1380